I0087433

A CourseGuide for

Basics of
Biblical
Hebrew

Gary D. Practico and
Miles V. Van Pelt

Z ZONDERVAN
ACADEMIC

ZONDERVAN ACADEMIC

A CourseGuide for Basics of Biblical Hebrew

Copyright © 2019 by Zondervan

ISBN 978-0-310-11110-8 (softcover)

Requests for information should be addressed to:
Zondervan, *3900 Sparks Dr. SE, Grand Rapids, Michigan 49546*

Printed in the United States of America

CONTENTS

Introduction

Welcome to *A CourseGuide for Basics of Biblical Hebrew*. These guides were created for formal and informal students alike who want to engage deeper in biblical, theological, or ministry studies. We hope this guide will provide an opportunity for you to grow not only in your understanding but also in your faith.

How to Use This Guide

This guide is meant to be used in conjunction with the book *Basics of Biblical Hebrew Grammar* and its corresponding videos, *Basics of Biblical Hebrew Video Lectures*. After you have read each chapter in the book and watched the accompanying video lesson, the materials in this guide will help you review and assess what you have learned. Application-oriented questions are included as well. For additional practice, you will want to complete the exercises found in *Basics of Biblical Hebrew Workbook*.

Each CourseGuide has been individually designed to best equip you in your studies, but in general, you can expect the following components. Most CourseGuides begin every chapter with a "You Should Know" section, which highlights key terminology, people, and facts to remember. This section serves as a helpful summary for directing your studies. Reflection questions, typically two to three per chapter, prompt you to summarize key points you've learned. Discussion questions invite you to an even deeper level of engagement. Finally, most chapters will end with a short quiz to test your retention. You can find the answer key to each quiz at the bottom of the page following it.

For Further Study

CourseGuides accompany books and videos from some of the world's top biblical and theological scholars. They may be used independently, or in small groups or classrooms, offering quality instruction to equip students for academic and ministry pursuits. If you would like to engage in further study with Zondervan's CourseGuides, the full lineup may be viewed online. After completing your studies with *A CourseGuide for Basics of Biblical Hebrew*, we recommend moving on to *A CourseGuide for Basics of Biblical Greek* and *A CourseGuide for Basics of Biblical Aramaic*.

Hebrew Alphabet and Vowels

You Should Know

- The Hebrew alphabet: א ב ג ד ה ו ז ח ט י כ ל מ נ ס ע פ צ ק ר ש ש ת

- Five letters of the Hebrew alphabet (פ, נ, מ, כ, and צ) have final forms (ף, ן, ם, ך, and ץ). These must be memorized.

- Six Hebrew consonants are known as *begadkephat* letters: בגדכפת. Each is capable of two different pronunciations, hard and soft. These pronunciations are distinguished by the presence or absence of a *Daghesh*. The distinction in pronunciation must be memorized.

- Four Hebrew consonants are called gutturals: ח, ה, א, and ע. Remember that ר may also behave like a guttural.

- Long, short, and reduced vowels are summarized in 2.6. Memorize the form, pronunciation, and name for each vowel symbol. You should also be able to give its vowel class (a, e, i, o, u) and vowel type (long, short, reduced).

- Vowel letters are summarized in 2.11. Memorize the form, pronunciation, and name for each vowel letter. You should also be able to give its vowel class (a, e, i, o, u).

- Vowel letters written with ה (He) occur only at the end of a word, as in תּוֹרָה (law) and יִבְנֶה (he will build).

- Vowel letters written with ו (Waw) and י (Yod) are often referred to as *unchangeable long vowels* because, as you will learn later, they do not reduce or "change."

- Defective writing is that phenomenon in which certain vowel letters are written without their consonant. There are three patterns of defective writing to be learned.

- The Daghesh Forte (בּ) doubles the consonant in which it appears. It can occur in any consonant except the gutturals and ר.

- אַבְרָהָם
  - Abraham

- אַהֲרֹן
  - Aaron

- דָּוִד
  - David

- יְהוּדָה
  - Judah

- יהוה
  - Yahweh

- יַעֲקֹב
  - Jacob

- יִצְחָק
  - Isaac

- יְרוּשָׁלַם
  - Jerusalem

Quiz

1. Select the correct representation of the biblical Hebrew alphabet.

   a) א ב ג ד ה ו ז ח ט י כ ל מ נ ס ע פ צ ק ר ש ת

   b) ת ש ש ר ק צ פ ע ס נ מ ל כ י ט ח ז ו ה ד ג ב א

   c) א ב ג ד ה ו ז ח ט י כ ל מ נ ס ע פ צ ק ר ש ת

   d) ת ש ש ר ק צ פ ע ס נ מ ל כ י ט ח ז ו ה ד ג ב א

2. The form of the final כ (Kaf) in Hebrew is

   a) ם
   b) ך
   c) ן
   d) ף

3. The form of the final מ (Mem) in Hebrew is

   a) ם
   b) ך
   c) ן
   d) ף

4. Final forms of the Hebrew consonants appear

   a) At the beginning of a word
   b) At the end of a word
   c) At the end of a sentence
   d) At the beginning of a quote

5. The *begadkephat* consonants are

   a) בגדכפת
   b) רעחהא
   c) צףןםך
   d) צסשש

6. Which of the following represents the names and symbols of all the Hebrew *Long Vowels*?

   a) Qamets (בָ), Seghol (בֶ), Holem (בֹ)
   b) Qamets (בָ), Seghol (בֶ), Holem (בֹו)
   c) Qamets (בָ), Tsere (בֵ), Holem (בֹ)
   d) Qamets (בָ), Tsere (בֵ), Holem (בֹ)

7. (T/F) The Hebrew long vowels can also be often called "changeable."

8. Which of the following represents the names and symbols of all the Hebrew *Short Vowels*?

   a) Pathach (בַ), Seghol (בֶ), Hireq (בִ), Holem Waw (בֹו), Qibbuts (בֻ)
   b) Pathach (בַ), Seghol (בֶ), Hireq (בִ), Qamets Hatuf (בָ), Qibbuts (בֻ)

c) Pathach (בַּ), Seghol (בֶּ), Hireq (בִּ), Holem Waw (בּוֹ), Qibbuts (בֻּ)

d) Pathach (בַּ), Seghol (בֶּ), Hireq (בִּ), Qamets Hatuf (בָּ), Qibbuts (בּוּ)

9. Which three consonants can also be written as *Vowel Letters*?

a) י ה ו

b) י ח ע

c) י ח ו

d) י ה א

10. Which of the following represents the names and symbols of all the Hebrew *Reduced Vowels*?

a) Hateph Pathach (בֲּ), Hateph Seghol (בֱּ), Hateph Holem (בְּוֹ)

b) Hateph Pathach (בֲּ), Hateph Seghol (בֱּ), Hateph Qamets (בֳּ)

c) Hateph Pathach (בֲּ), Hateph Hireq (בֱּ), Hateph Qamets (בֳּ)

d) Hateph Pathach (בֲּ), Hateph Seghol (בֱּ), Hateph Qamets (בֳּ)

CHAPTER 3

Syllabification and Pronunciation

You Should Know

- אָב
  - father, ancestor

- אָדוֹן
  - lord, master

- אָדָם
  - man, humankind

- אֲדָמָה
  - land, earth, ground

- אָח
  - brother

- אָחוֹת
  - sister, relative, loved one

- אִישׁ
  - man, husband

- אֵל
  - God, god

- אֱלֹהִים
  - God, gods

- אֵם
  - mother

- Every syllable must begin with a consonant and have only one vowel (with very few exceptions).

- There are only two types of syllables: open and closed. Open syllables end with a vowel and closed syllables end with a consonant.

- A *Daghesh Forte* doubles the consonant in which it occurs and must be divided in syllabification.

- A *Daghesh* in a *begadkephat* consonant is a *Lene* if preceded by a consonant and a *Forte* if preceded by a vowel.

- A *Daghesh Forte* in a *begadkephat* consonant doubles the hard sound and not the soft sound.

- The gutturals and ר cannot take *Daghesh Lene* or *Daghesh Forte*.

Quiz

1. (T/F) Every syllable must begin with one consonant and may have more than one vowel.

2. Open syllables end with a ____ and closed syllables end with a ____.
   - a) Vowel, Silent Shewa
   - b) Daghesh Forte, Consonant
   - c) Vowel, Consonant
   - d) Vocal Shewa, Silent Shewa

3. Hebrew words are usually accented on which syllable?
   - a) Tonic
   - b) Last
   - c) First
   - d) Closed

4. Consider the word דְּ | בָ | רִים. What is the correct classification of the דְּ syllable (1), the בָ syllable (2), and the רִים syllable (3)?
   - a) (1) Propretonic (2) Pretonic (3) Tonic
   - b) (1) Tonic (2) Pretonic (3) Propretonic
   - c) (1) Pretonic (2) Open (3) Closed
   - d) (1) Closed (2) Open (3) Tonic

5. Which of the following statements regarding syllabification of the Daghesh Forte are correct?

(1) Doubles the value of a consonant (2) A vertical line is drawn through the consonant containing it (3) Always hardens the consonant which it is in (4) Begins a syllable (5) Ends a syllable

    a) 1, 2, 3, 4
    b) 2, 3, 4, 5
    c) 1, 3, 4, 5
    d) 1, 2, 4, 5

6. (T/F) A Daghesh in a *begadkephat* consonant is a Forte if preceded by a vowel and is a Lene if preceded by a consonant.

7. A Shewa is silent if the previous vowel is:

    a) Long
    b) Beneath a guttural
    c) Short
    d) Beneath a *begadkephat* consonant

8. (T/F) The Qamets Hatuf occurs only in an *open and unaccented* syllable.

9. Which consonants does a *Furtive Pathach* appear under, and when do you pronounce it?

    a) א and ה; before the guttural
    b) א and ה; after the guttural
    c) ח and ע; before the guttural
    d) ח and ע; after the guttural

10. In וַיֹּאמֶר, the א is said to be ___ since it has no vowel.

    a) Unaccented
    b) Silent
    c) Quiescent
    d) Diphthong

ANSWER KEY

1. F, 2. C, 3. B, 4. A, 5. D, 6. T, 7. C, 8. F, 9. C, 10. C

CHAPTER 4

Hebrew Nouns

You Should Know

- גּוֹי
  - nation, people

- דֶּרֶךְ
  - way, road, journey

- הַר
  - mountain, hill, hill country

- כֹּהֵן
  - priest

- לֵב
  - heart, mind, will

- מַיִם
  - water

- מֶלֶךְ
  - king, ruler

- נָבִיא
  - prophet

- נֶפֶשׁ
  - soul, life, person, neck, throat

- סוּס
  - horse

- Hebrew nouns have both *gender* and *number*. With regard to gender, a noun will be either *masculine* or *feminine*, rarely both. With regard to number, a noun will be *singular*, *plural*, or *dual*.

- Masculine singular nouns are endingless. Masculine plural nouns take the ים ending. Masculine dual nouns take the יִם ending.

- The most common feminine singular ending is ה ָ, but several other endings with ת also occur (וּת / ת ֶ / ית / ת ַ). Feminine plural nouns take the ending וֹת. Feminine dual nouns take the יִם or תַיִם ending. Feminine singular nouns that end in ה ָ will not be identified as feminine in the vocabulary sections or in the grammar's lexicon.

- Exceptions to these standard rules or patterns include:
  - *Endless Feminine Nouns*. All masculine singular nouns are endingless, but a few feminine singular nouns are also endingless.
  - *Exception to Normal Pluralization*. A few singular nouns of one gender take the plural endings of the other gender.
  - *Special Dual Nouns*. A few nouns are always dual in form but usually singular in meaning.
  - *Irregular Stem Change*. A few nouns change their (consonantal) stem when forming the plural.
  - Defective Spelling of וֹת. Sometimes, the feminine plural ending וֹת will be spelled with a Holem rather than a Holem Waw.

- Most nouns undergo a change in vowel pattern with the addition of plural endings. Be certain that you learn the patterns of noun pluralization that are discussed in section 4.8.

- A Hebrew dictionary is called a *lexicon*. When looking up words you must search for them by their *lexical form*. The lexical form of a Hebrew noun is the *singular form*.

Quiz

1. (T/F) With regard to number, a noun can either be singular, masculine, or dual.

2. Pluralize the noun אָב.

   a) אָבִים
   b) אָבוֹת
   c) אֲבִים
   d) אֲבֹתִים

3. The most common feminine singular ending is

   a) ָה
   b) וּת
   c) ִית
   d) ָת

4. (T/F) All Masculine Singular nouns are endingless, but not all endingless nouns are Masculine Singular.

5. Pluralize the noun אִשָּׁה.

   a) אֲנָשִׁים
   b) אִשּׁוֹת
   c) נָשׁוֹת
   d) נָשִׁים

6. In an open, propretonic syllable, what happens to a Qamets or Tsere (Propretonic Reduction)?

   a) Reduces to its class-corresponding Hateph vowel (guttural)
   b) Reduces to Vocal Shewa
   c) Reduces to Silent Shewa
   d) Both A and B

7. All two-syllable nouns that are accented on the first syllable are

   a) Biconsonantal Nouns
   b) Geminate Nouns
   c) Segholate Nouns
   d) Tonic Nouns

8. Which example of the Plural word מֶלֶךְ represents the Segholate noun pluralization pattern?

   a) מְלָכִים
   b) מֶלָכִים

c) מְלָכִים

d) מְלֵכִים

9. When a Geminate noun is pluralized, what happens to the original Geminate consonant?

a) reappears as a Daghesh Forte (עַמִּים)
b) reappears as a Daghesh Lene (עַמִּים)
c) simply reappears (עַמְמִים)
d) disappears (עַמִים)

10. The lexical form of a Hebrew noun is its

a) Singular Form
b) Plural Form
c) Dual Form
d) Feminine Form

CHAPTER 5

Definitive Article and Conjunction Waw

You Should Know

- אֵשׁ
  - fire
- הֵיכָל
  - temple
- זָהָב
  - gold
- חֶרֶב
  - sword
- יֶלֶד
  - child, boy, youth
- יָם
  - sea
- כֶּסֶף
  - silver, money
- מִזְבֵּחַ
  - altar
- מָקוֹם
  - place, location
- מִשְׁפָּט
  - judgment, decision, ordinance, law, custom

- In general, the Hebrew definite article *functions* much like the English definite article. There is no indefinite article in Hebrew.

- A noun is made definite by prefixing the definite article, which consists of ה plus the Daghesh Forte in the first consonant of the noun to which it is prefixed.

- There are several other spelling possibilities for the article depending on the spelling of the word to which it is prefixed.

  - The Daghesh Lene of an initial *begadkephat* consonant becomes a Daghesh Forte with the prefixing of the definite article.

  - With initial א, ע, and ר, the rejection of the Daghesh Forte results in *compensatory lengthening*—the lengthening of the Pathach to a Qamets.

  - With initial ה and ח, the Daghesh Forte is rejected, but the Pathach does not lengthen. This is *virtual doubling*.

  - When nouns begin with unaccented הָ, חָ, or עָ (עָ may also be accented), the definite article appears with an irregular Seghol vowel and without the Daghesh Forte.

  - Words that begin with י or מ can give up the Daghesh Forte that is associated with the definite article. The loss of the Daghesh Forte is governed by the rule of sqnmlwy.

- The Hebrew conjunction ו (and, but, also, even) is the most frequently occurring word in the Hebrew Bible. It is always prefixed to the word that follows.

Quiz

1. In Hebrew, a noun is made definite by prefixing the definite article, which consists of

    a) הַ plus a *Daghesh Lene* (הַמֶּלֶךְ)

    b) הָ plus a *Daghesh Forte* (הָמֶּלֶךְ)

    c) הַ plus a *Daghesh Forte* (הַמֶּלֶךְ)

    d) הָ plus a *Daghesh Lene* (הָמֶּלֶךְ)

2. הָרֹאשׁ has the definite article prefixed to it. What is the form an example of?

   a) Virtual Doubling

   b) *sknmlwy*

   c) Compensatory Lengthening

   d) Segholization

3. Which consonants experience *compensatory lengthening* when prefixed with the definite article?

   a) א ר ע

   b) ה ר ע

   c) א ח ר

   d) ה ח א

4. Which of the following motivates *virtual doubling* when prefixed with the definite article?

   a) ח ה י מָ

   b) א ה י מָ

   c) ח ה

   d) א ה

5. The definite article will appear as הַ when followed by

   a) אַ הָ חַ

   b) אָ הָ חָ

   c) עַ הָ חַ

   d) עָ הָ חָ

6. Before ב מ פ and consonants with Vocal Shewa, the *conjunction waw* will appear as

   a) Hireq Waw (וִ)

   b) Shureq (וּ)

   c) Holem Waw (וֹ)

   d) Waw with Qamets (וָ)

7. Prefix the *conjunction waw* to אֱמֶת.

   a) וָאֱמֶת

   b) וֶאֱמֶת

c) וֶאֱמֶת

d) וֶאֱמֶת

8. Prefix the *conjunction waw* to לֶחֶם.

    a) וְלֶחֶם

    b) וִלֶחֶם

    c) וֻלֶחֶם

    d) וֹלֶחֶם

9. Identify the lexical form of the *conjunction waw*.

    a) וְ

    b) וֶ

    c) וּ

    d) וָ

10. Translate: וְהָאִשָּׁה

    a) And the man

    b) And a man

    c) And the woman

    d) And a woman

CHAPTER 6

Hebrew Prepositions

You Should Know

- אַחֲרֵי
  - after, behind
- אֶל־
  - to, toward, into
- אֵת (prep)
  - with, beside
- בְּ
  - in, at, with, by, against
- כְּ
  - as, like, according to
- לְ
  - to, toward, for
- בֵּין
  - between
- בְּתוֹךְ
  - in the midst (middle) of, inside
- כֹּל
  - all, each, every
- לְמַעַן
  - on account of, for the sake of

- Hebrew prepositions function like English prepositions. The word following the preposition is called the *object* of the preposition.

- There are three types of Hebrew prepositions: independent, Maqqef, and inseparable.

Independent prepositions stand alone. Maqqef prepositions are joined to their objects by a raised horizontal stroke called *Maqqef*. Inseparable prepositions are prefixed directly to their objects.

- The inseparable prepositions בְּ (in, by, with), כְּ (like, as, according to), and לְ (to, for) are prefixed directly to their objects and never occur independently.
    - Before most consonants, the inseparable prepositions will appear with Vocal Shewa as כְּ, בְּ, or לְ.
    - Before a reduced or Hateph vowel, the inseparable prepositions are spelled with the corresponding short vowel of the Hateph vowel.
    - Before consonants with Vocal Shewa, the inseparable prepositions are spelled with Hireq because of the application of Rule of Shewa (4.11.1).
    - In nouns with the definite article, the vowel and Daghesh Forte of the definite article are retained, but the consonant of the preposition replaces the ה of the definite article.

- The preposition מִן occurs both as a Maqqef preposition and as an inseparable preposition. When occurring as an inseparable preposition, the נ assimilates into the following consonant and appears as a Daghesh Forte. This Daghesh Forte is rejected by gutturals, resulting in either compensatory lengthening or virtual doubling.

- The preposition מִן can be used comparatively (better than); superlatively with מִכֹּל (כֹּל, the most); or partitively (some of).

- In Hebrew prose, definite direct objects are usually marked with אֶת/אֵת־ (the accusative marker). The definite direct object marker is never translated. It is a word that has a grammatical function but no translation value.

Quiz

1. Which of the following prepositions are said to be *inseparable*?

   a) בְּ
   b) לְ
   c) כְּ
   d) All of the above

2. How would you prefix the לְ preposition to the word חֲלִי?

   a) לְחֲלִי
   b) לֶחֳלִי
   c) לַחֲלִי
   d) לַחֳלִי

3. Which of the following examples represents the correct way to prefix a preposition to a *definite* noun?

   a) בְּהַשָּׂדֶה
   b) בַּשָּׂדֶה
   c) בְּ־שָׂדֶה
   d) בְּשָׂדֶה

4. (T/F) The preposition מִן can occur either as a Maqqef preposition or an inseparable preposition.

5. Translate: כְּמֶּלֶךְ

   a) Like a king
   b) For the king
   c) Like the king
   d) For a king

6. When used as an inseparable preposition, what happens to the spelling of מִן?

   a) The Nun (נ) drops the Maqqef and adds a vocal shewa (מְנבַּיִת)
   b) The Nun (נ) assimilates in the following consonant as a *Daghesh Forte* (מִבַּיִת)
   c) The Nun (נ) assimilates in the following consonant as a *Daghesh Lene* (מִבַּיִת)
   d) The Nun (נ) drops the Maqqef and adds a silent shewa (מְנבַּיִת)

7. (T/F) The three uses of מִן are the Comparative, the Superlative, and the Indicative.

8. What is the use of the word אֵת/אֶת־?
   a) Marks a direct object
   b) Marks an indirect object
   c) Marks a definite direct object
   d) Marks a definite indirect object

9. Translate: שָׁמַע (He heard) אֶת־הַדְּבָרִים מִן־הַמֶּלֶךְ
   a) He heard words from the king
   b) He heard the words from the king
   c) He heard the word from a king
   d) He heard a word from the king

10. (T/F) The three types of Hebrew prepositions are independent, dependent, and inseparable.

CHAPTER 7

Hebrew Adjectives

You Should Know

- קֹדֶשׁ
  - holiness, something that is holy

- רָעָה
  - evil, wickedness, calamity, disaster

- גָּדוֹל
  - great, big, large

- זָקֵן
  - old; (n) elder, old man

- זָר
  - foreign, strange

- חַי
  - living, alive

- חָכָם
  - wise, skillful, experienced

- טוֹב
  - good, pleasant

- יָשָׁר
  - upright, just

- מְעַט
  - little, few

- Hebrew adjectives inflect in order to indicate gender and number. They are inflected in four forms: masculine singular and masculine plural, feminine singular and feminine plural. The inflectional endings for adjectives are the same endings that you have already learned for nouns.

- Hebrew adjectives agree in gender and number with the nouns they modify. The gender of an adjective does not change the meaning of an adjective.

- Adjectives that are plural in form are singular in translation value. The number of an adjective does not change the translation value of an adjective.

- Be certain that you know and understand the basic patterns of adjectival inflection described in 7.4.

- Adjectival usage falls into three categories: attributive, predicative, and substantive.

  - *Attributive* adjectives follow the noun they modify and agree in gender, number, and definiteness (or indefiniteness).

  - *Predicative* adjectives either precede or follow the noun they modify and agree in gender and number only. Predicative adjectives never take the definite article.

  - *Substantive* adjectives are used independently as nouns. In this usage, there will be no noun for the adjective to modify.

- In Hebrew, the directional ending הָ may be added to the end of a word in order to express the idea of motion toward someone or something. The directional ending is always unaccented and is translated "to" or "toward."

Quiz

1. (T/F) Hebrew adjectives agree with the noun they modify in gender, number, and definiteness.

2. Which of the following is true of *Attributive* adjectives?

    a) Modifies its noun

    b) Agrees with its noun only in gender and number

    c) Comes before the noun it modifies

    d) All of the above

3. (T/F) The *Predicative* use of the adjective asserts something about a noun and agrees in gender and number but *not* definiteness.

4. Translate: הָאִישׁ טוֹב

    a) A good man

    b) The good man

    c) A man is good

    d) The man is good

    e) A or C, depending on context

5. *Substantive* adjectives function

    a) Like Attributive adjectives

    b) Like Predicative adjectives

    c) Like nouns

    d) Any of the above

6. Translate: אִשָּׁה טוֹבָה

    a) The good woman

    b) The woman is good

    c) A good woman

    d) A woman is good

    e) C or D, depending on context

7. Translate: מִצְרַיְמָה

    a) Egypt (masculine)

    b) Egypt (feminine)

    c) To Egypt

    d) From Egypt

8. Translate: חָכָם

    a) Wise

    b) The wise one

    c) Wisely

    d) None of the above

9. What is the *feminine singular* ending for adjectives?

    a) הָ

    b) וֹת

    c) הֶ

    d) הִ

10. (T/F) The gender of an adjective changes the meaning of an adjective.

CHAPTER 8

Hebrew Pronouns

You Should Know

- אַחֵר
  - other, another
- אֵלֶּה
  - these
- אֲשֶׁר
  - who, that, which
- אַתָּה
  - you (ms pronoun)
- אֲנַחְנוּ
  - we
- אֲנִי
  - I
- אָנֹכִי
  - I
- אַתֶּם
  - you (mp pronoun)
- הַ
  - interrogative particle
- הוּא
  - he, it

- A pronoun is a word that replaces a noun. The noun that the pronoun refers back to is called the *antecedent*.

- A *personal pronoun* is a pronoun that replaces a noun referring to a person or thing. It can be first, second, or third person and either singular or plural. First person pronouns are labeled "common," meaning that they may refer to either masculine or feminine nouns (they are not inflected for gender). Second and third person pronouns have both masculine and feminine forms. The independent personal pronouns and their translations, as presented in 8.3 in the grammar, must be memorized.

- The Hebrew demonstratives may be used as either adjectives (*this* man, *those* women) or pronouns (*this* is the man, *those* are the women). The demonstratives and their translations, as presented in 8.6 in the grammar, must be memorized.

  - When a Hebrew demonstrative is functioning as an adjective, it will *follow* the noun it modifies and agree in gender, number, *and definiteness*.

  - When a Hebrew demonstrative is functioning as a pronoun, it will *precede* the noun it modifies and agree in gender and number *but not definiteness*.

  - The word אֲשֶׁר (who, whom, whose, which, that) functions as the Hebrew relative pronoun. The form of this word never changes.

  - In Hebrew, the most common interrogative pronouns are מִי (who? whom?) and מָה (what?). These words do not inflect and can appear with or without the Maqqef.

  - Another way Hebrew creates a question is with the interrogative particle הֲ. This particle is prefixed to the first word of the interrogative clause. Usually, it is spelled הֲ. However, it also occurs as הַ (before most guttural consonants and consonants with Shewa) and הֶ (before guttural consonants with Qamets).

Quiz

1. Identify the correct use of the Hebrew independent personal pronoun.

    a) Subjective
    b) Predicative
    c) Both A and B
    d) None of the above

2. Translate: אֲנַחְנוּ אַחִים
    a) We are the brothers
    b) The brothers are ours
    c) We are brothers
    d) We are our brothers

3. (T/F) First person personal pronouns are *common* with reference to gender.

4. What way(s) can the demonstratives be used?
    a) Definite article
    b) Demonstrative adjective
    c) Independent personal pronoun
    d) None of the above

5. Translate: הָאִישׁ הַטּוֹב הַזֶּה
    a) That good man
    b) This good man
    c) That man is good
    d) This man is good

6. (T/F) When a Hebrew demonstrative is functioning as a pronoun, it will *precede* the noun and agree in gender and number but not definiteness.

7. Translate: זֶה הָאִישׁ הַטּוֹב
    a) This is the good man
    b) This man is good
    c) That man is good
    d) That is the good man

8. How does the Hebrew word אֲשֶׁר function?
    a) As a demonstrative
    b) As an adjective

c) As an independent personal pronoun

d) As a relative pronoun

9. How would you write "the mountains that are under the heavens?"

a) הָרִים אֲשֶׁר־תַּחַת הַשָּׁמָיִם

b) הֶהָרִים אֲשֶׁר־תַּחַת הַשָּׁמָיִם

c) אֲשֶׁר הֶהָרִים תַּחַת הַשָּׁמָיִם

d) הֶהָרִים אֲשֶׁר־תַּחַת שָׁמָיִם

10. Which of the following statements helps you distinguish between the definite article (הַ + Daghesh Forte) and the interrogative particle (הֲ)?

a) The *Hateph Pathach* is not one of the spellings of the definite article

b) The interrogative particle is usually fixed to verbs or other particles whereas the definite article is not

c) The interrogative particle does not have a Daghesh Forte associated with it

d) All of the above

CHAPTER 9

Hebrew Pronominal Suffixes

You Should Know

- אַף
  - nostril, nose; (metaphorically) anger
- בָּקָר
  - cattle, herd
- בֹּקֶר
  - morning
- בְּרָכָה
  - blessing, gift
- חַטָּאת
  - sin, sin offering
- כָּבוֹד
  - glory, splendor, honor, abundance
- כְּלִי
  - vessel, implement, weapon
- לֶחֶם
  - bread, food
- מִלְחָמָה
  - war, battle, struggle
- מִשְׁפָּחָה
  - family, clan

- Pronominal suffixes are *possessive* (my, his, her) when appearing on nouns and *objective* (me, him, her) when appearing on prepositions.

- All pronominal suffixes have person, gender, and number.

- There are two sets of pronominal suffixes to be learned, Type 1 (for singular nouns and select prepositions) and Type 2 (for plural nouns and select prepositions). Both types have the same possessive and objective translation values. As a general observation, Type 2 suffixes are distinguished by the presence of י throughout their spelling.

- The dot in the Type 1 3fs suffix is called *Mappiq* (הּ). It is neither the Daghesh Forte nor the Daghesh Lene.

- Singular nouns can take both singular and plural pronominal suffixes. Plural nouns can also take both singular and plural pronominal suffixes.

- Certain singular monosyllabic nouns will add י to their stem before a pronominal suffix.

- Prepositions may take either Type 1 or Type 2 pronominal suffixes. Which type of suffix a preposition prefers is of little significance because the translation value is the same for both types.

- With the addition of pronominal suffixes, the prepositions כְּ (like, as, according to) and מִן (from) exhibit longer, alternate spellings with singular and 1cp suffixes.

- The object marker אֶת־/אֵת takes Type 1 pronominal suffixes. It is translated as a personal pronoun in the objective or accusative case. Be careful not to confuse the object marker with the preposition.

Quiz

1. (T/F) Usually, Type 1 suffixes will occur with plural nouns and Type 2 suffixes will occur with singular nouns.

2. How would you write "my horses" in Hebrew?

a) סוּסִימִי

b) סוּסִי

c) סוּסִימִי

d) סוּסִי

3. Translate: שָׂדְךָ

   a) Your field (2ms)
   b) Your field (2fs)
   c) Your fields (2ms)
   d) Your fields (2fs)

4. What happens to feminine nouns ending in ◌ָה before receiving a pronominal suffix?

   a) Qamets is replaced by Seghol (◌ֶה)
   b) The feminine plural ending is used (וֹת)
   c) He is replaced by Taw (◌ַת)
   d) Nothing happens

5. (T/F) Certain singular monosyllabic nouns will add י to their stem before taking a pronominal suffix.

6. Correctly identify, in order, the full Type 1 Suffix paradigm with the preposition לְ.

   a) לִי לְךָ לָךְ לוֹ לָהּ לָנוּ לָכֶם לָכֶן לָהֶם לָהֶן
   b) לִי לְךָ לָךְ לוֹ לָהּ לָנוּ לָכֶם לָכֶם לָהֶם לָהֶן
   c) לִי לְךָ לָךְ לוֹ לָהּ לָנוּ לָכֶם לָכֶן לָהֶם לָהֶן
   d) לִי לְךָ לָךְ לוֹ לָהּ לָנוּ לָכֶן לָכֶם לָהֶם לָהֶן

7. When a pronominal suffix is fixed to a preposition it is

   a) Subjective
   b) Objective
   c) Possessive
   d) None of the above

8. Translate: כָּמוֹנִי

   a) Like us
   b) For us
   c) Like me
   d) For me

9. Translate: אִתָּךְ

    a) With you (2ms)

    b) With you (2fs)

    c) You (2ms)

    d) You (2fs)

10. What is the name of the dot in the Type 1 3fs Suffix (ה)?

    a) Daghesh Forte

    b) Daghesh Lene

    c) Mappiq

    d) Maqqef

CHAPTER 10

Hebrew Construct Chain

You Should Know

- אֶבֶן
  - stone

- אֹיֵב
  - enemy

- בְּרִית
  - covenant

- בָּשָׂר
  - flesh, meat, skin

- גְּבוּל
  - border, boundary, territory

- חֹדֶשׁ
  - month, new moon

- חַיִל
  - strength, wealth, army

- חֶסֶד
  - loyalty, faithfulness, steadfast love, lovingkindness

- יָד
  - hand

- מִדְבָּר
  - wilderness, desert, pasture

- Hebrew expresses the "of" (possessive) relationship between two nouns by placing them side by side, in a *construct chain*. In a construct chain, there is only one absolute noun and the absolute noun is always the last noun in the chain. Multiple construct nouns may appear in a construct chain.

- Basic Grammar of the Hebrew Construct Chain.

  - Nouns in a construct chain may be linked by Maqqef.

  - Construct chains are either definite (*the ... of the ...*) or indefinite (*a ... of a ...*). The definiteness or indefiniteness of a construct chain is determined by the definiteness or indefiniteness of the absolute noun. The construct noun will not take the definite article. Therefore, a construct chain is definite if the absolute noun is definite, and indefinite if the absolute noun is indefinite.

  - Although a construct noun cannot take the definite article, a construct noun may appear with one of the inseparable prepositions.

  - When two or more nouns are in construct, no other words or particles may separate them. For this reason, an attributive or demonstrative adjective must follow the construct chain while still agreeing in gender, number, and definiteness with the noun that it modifies.

- When a noun appears in the construct state, it surrenders its primary accent to the absolute noun and the entire construct chain is treated as a single accented unit. The types of spelling changes encountered with most construct nouns can be grouped into two basic categories: (1) vowel reduction; and (2) a change in the ending of a construct noun.

Quiz

1. → עֶבֶד הַמֶּלֶךְ; The arrow here is pointing to the ...

   a) Construct Noun
   b) Absolute Noun

    c) Independent Personal Pronoun

    d) None of the above

2. (T/F) A Hebrew construct chain can only have one absolute noun and one construct noun.

3. (T/F) If two nouns are "in construct," no other words or particles may separate them.

4. Translate: קוֹל הָאִישׁ

    a) A voice of the man

    b) The voice of the man

    c) A voice of a man

    d) The voice of a man

5. Translate: סֵפֶר אָבִיהוּ

    a) The book of his father

    b) The book of our father

    c) A book of his father

    d) A book of our father

6. If an attributive or demonstrative adjective is added to a construct chain, where must it be written?

    a) Before the construct chain

    b) After the construct chain

    c) Its appropriate place is before or after the noun

    d) None of the above

7. Translate: קְדוֹשׁ יִשְׂרָאֵל

    a) The Holy One of Israel

    b) Israel is holy

    c) Holy Israel

    d) Israel of holiness

8. (T/F) A common spelling change encountered with construct nouns is vowel reduction.

9. What is the masculine plural ending for nouns in the construct state?

a) יִם.

b) הָ

c) יִ.

d) יְ.

10. (T/F) Certain singular monosyllabic nouns will add Hireq Yod (יִ) to their stem when in the construct state.

CHAPTER 11

Hebrew Numbers

You Should Know

- אֶחָד
  - one
- שְׁנַיִם
  - two
- שָׁלֹשׁ
  - three
- אַרְבַּע
  - four
- חָמֵשׁ
  - five
- שֵׁשׁ
  - six
- שֶׁבַע
  - seven
- שְׁמֹנֶה
  - eight
- תֵּשַׁע
  - nine
- עֶשֶׂר
  - ten

- Cardinal numbers are used for counting (one, two, three, etc.), and ordinal numbers are used to indicate position in a series (first, second, third, etc.).

- In Hebrew, cardinal numbers have both masculine and feminine forms. They also occur in the absolute and construct states. In most instances, you need only to memorize the masculine absolute forms.

- While the cardinal number one functions like an adjective, numbers two and higher function like nouns. Note that numbers three through ten do not agree in gender with the noun with which they are associated.

- Cardinal numbers eleven through nineteen are formed with a combination of the number ten and one through nine.

- In Hebrew, the number twenty-one and other such numbers occur as either "twenty and one" or, less frequently, as "one and twenty."

Quiz

1. The Hebrew number one (אֶחָד) is used like a(n)
    a) Noun
    b) Adverb
    c) Adjective
    d) None of the above

2. Translate: אַחַד הַבָּנִים
    a) One son
    b) The one son
    c) One of the sons
    d) The only son

3. (T/F) The Hebrew number two (שְׁנַיִם) is classified as a noun.

4. Translate: שְׁנֵיהֶם
    a) Two of them (3fp)
    b) Two of them (3mp)
    c) Twice
    d) Second

5. How are cardinal numbers eleven through nineteen written?

   a) Ten plus one through nine
   b) One through nine plus ten
   c) Either A or B
   d) None of the above

6. Translate: שְׁנֵי עָשָׂר אִישׁ

   a) Two that are men
   b) Those twelve men
   c) Twelve men
   d) The twelve men

7. What do you add to turn ten (עֶשֶׂר) to twenty, three (שָׁלֹשׁ) to thirty, etc.?

   a) ִים
   b) ָה
   c) ְים
   d) ֶה

8. Translate: שְׁלֹשׁ מֵאוֹת

   a) 103
   b) 300
   c) 3,000
   d) 1,003

9. How do you write the Hebrew ordinal "first?"

   a) רֹאשׁ
   b) רִאשׁוֹן
   c) אֶחָדִי
   d) רֹאשִׁי

10. The masculine ordinals second through tenth end in

   a) ִים
   b) ִי
   c) ְים
   d) ָה

CHAPTER 12

Introduction to Hebrew Verbs

You Should Know

- אָכַל
  - (Q) to eat, consume; (Ni) be eaten, consumed; (Hi) feed

- אָמַר
  - (Q) to say; (Ni) be said, called; (Hi) declare, proclaim

- הָיָה
  - (Q) to be, become, happen, occur; (Ni) be done, brought about, come to pass, occur

- הָלַךְ
  - (Q) to go, walk, (metaphorically) behave; (Pi) go, walk; (Hith) walk about, move to and fro

- יָצָא
  - (Q) to go or come out; (Hi) cause to go or come out, lead out, bring out

- יָשַׁב
  - (Q) to sit (down), dwell, inhabit; (Hi) cause to sit or dwell, settle (a city)

- נָגַשׁ
  - (Q) to draw near, approach; (Ni) draw near; (Hi) bring (near), offer

- נָתַן
  - (Q) to give, put, place, set; (Ni) be given

- עָשָׂה
  - (Q) to do, make; (Ni) be done, made

- רָאָה
  - (Q) to see, perceive, understand; (Ni) appear; (Pu) be seen; (Hi) let or cause someone to see (something)

- Verbs are those words used to describe an action or state of being.

- A *root* represents the origin or simplest form from which any number of Hebrew words are derived. Most Hebrew roots are triconsonantal.

- Hebrew verbs can indicate person, gender, and number by certain patterns of *inflection*.

- Hebrew verbs may appear in seven different *stems*: the Qal and six derived stems (Niphal, Piel, Pual, Hiphil, Hophal, Hithpael). These stems indicate verbal action (simple, intensive, causative) and verbal voice (active, passive, reflexive).

- Hebrew verbs may be inflected in six different conjugations: Perfect (suffix), Imperfect (prefix), Imperative, Infinitive Construct, Infinitive Absolute, and Participle. The term "conjugation" is used to describe the verbal forms that express different verbal functions.

- Hebrew verbs are classified as either *strong* or *weak*. Weak verbs are those verbs having at least one weak root consonant. Strong verbs have no weak consonants.

- Though frequent exceptions and variations do exist, the normal word order for a Hebrew verbal sentence is *verb-subject-object*.

- The process of "parsing" a verb involves the identification of the verbal stem, conjugation, person, gender, number, and lexical form with vowels or verbal roots without vowels.

- The lexical form of a triconsonantal verb is the *Qal Perfect 3ms*.

Quiz

1. How many consonants does a Hebrew root *typically* have?

    a) 2

    b) 3

    c) 4

    d) 5

2. What does any given ending on a Hebrew verb indicate?

    a) Person, Gender

    b) Person, Gender, Number

    c) Gender, Number

    d) Person, Number

3. What is indicated by a Hebrew *stem*?

    a) The type of verbal action

    b) The voice of verbal action

    c) The voice and type of verbal action

    d) The relationship between the verbal action and the subject

4. Correctly identify the three most basic categories of Hebrew verbal *action*.

    a) Simple, Passive, Active

    b) Simple, Intensive, Causative

    c) Active, Passive, Reflexive

    d) Active, Intensive, Causative

5. Correctly identify the three most basic categories of Hebrew verbal *voice*.

    a) Simple, Passive, Active

    b) Simple, Intensive, Causative

    c) Active, Passive, Reflexive

    d) Active, Intensive, Causative

6. The *stem vowel* is associated with which consonant of the verbal root?

    a) First

    b) Second

    c) Third

    d) Consonant before the added ending

7. I-Guttural, II-Guttural, III-ע/ח, III-א, Biconsonantal, etc. are all examples of

    a) Strong verbal roots

    b) Weak verbal roots

    c) Doubly weak verbal

    d) Doubly strong verbal roots

8. What is typical Hebrew word order?

    a) Object-Verb-Subject

    b) Verb-Object-Subject

    c) Verb-Subject-Object

    d) Subject-Verb-Object

9. (T/F) Parsing is the process whereby you identify a verb's stem, conjugation, person, number, and lexical form *only*.

10. What is the lexical form of a triconsonantal verb?

    a) Qal Perfect 2fs

    b) Qal Imperfect 3ms

    c) Qal Perfect 3ms

    d) Qal Perfect

CHAPTER 13

Qal Perfect Strong Verbs

You Should Know

- בָּרַךְ
  - (Q Pass ptc) blessed, praised, adored; (Pi) bless, praise

- זָכַר
  - (Q) to remember; (Ni) be remembered, thought of; (Hi) remind

- חָזַק
  - (Q) to be(come) strong, have courage; (Pi) make strong, strengthen; (Hi) strengthen, seize, grasp, take hold of; (Hith) strengthen oneself, show oneself as strong or courageous

- יָדַע
  - (Q) to know, know sexually (have intercourse with); (Ni) be(come) known, reveal oneself; (Hi) make known, inform

- כָּבֵד
  - (Q) to be heavy, weighty, honored; (Ni) be honored; (Pi) honor; (Hi) make heavy, dull or insensitive, harden (heart)

- כָּתַב
  - (Q) to write (upon), register, record; (Ni) be written

- מָלֵא
  - (Q) to be full, fill (up); (Ni) be filled (with); (Pi) fill, perform, carry out, consecrate as priest

- מָצָא
  - (Q) to find (out), reach, obtain, achieve; (Ni) be found

- פָּקַד
  - (Q) to attend (to), pay attention to, take care of, miss (someone), number, appoint; (Ni) be missed, visited, appointed; (Hi) appoint, entrust

- שָׁכַב
  - (Q) to lie down, have sexual intercourse (with)

- The Qal stem is the simple or basic verbal stem. It is used to express *simple action* with an *active voice*.

- The simple action of the Qal stem may be *transitive* (can take a direct object), *intransitive* (cannot take a direct object), or *stative* (describing a state of being).

- The Perfect conjugation is used to express a *completed action* and is translated with the English past tense (also with the English present perfect, past perfect, and future perfect tenses). It may also be used to describe a *state of being* and, as such, will be translated with the English past or present tense.

- The Perfect conjugation is also called the "suffix conjugation" because different inflectional endings or *sufformatives* are added to the verbal root in order to indicate person, gender, and number.

- You must memorize the Qal Perfect paradigm of the strong verb. You must also memorize the Perfect sufformatives.

- When a verbal root ending in ת receives a sufformative beginning with ת, the two identical consonants become one consonant with Daghesh Forte.

- Perfect (and Imperfect) verbs are negated with the particle לֹא. This particle is always placed immediately before the verb

Quiz

1. (T/F) The Qal Stem is used to express *simple action* with an *active voice*.

2. Stative verbs

   a) May take a direct object

   b) State something about the subject

   c) Describe a state of being

   d) May not take a direct object

3. (T/F) The perfect conjugation is used to express a completed action, and may *only* be translated in the past tense.

4. What is the name of the endings added to the verbal root?

   a) Preformatives

   b) Sufformatives

   c) Pronominal

   d) None of the above

5. Correctly identify the vowel pattern for the Qal Perfect 3ms Strong Verb.

   a) קֶטַל

   b) קֹטֵל

   c) קָטַל

   d) קָטֶל

6. Correctly identify, in the order presented in *BBH*, the Qal Perfect Paradigm of the Strong Verb.

   a) קָטַל קָֽטְלָה קָטַלְתָּ קָטַלְתְּ קָטַלְתִּי קָֽטְלוּ קְטַלְתֶּם קְטַלְתֶּן קָטַֽלְנוּ

   b) קָטַל קָֽטְלָה קָטַלְתָּ קָטַלְתְּ קָטַלְתִּי קָֽטְלוּ קְטַלְתֶּם קְטַלְתֶּן קָטַֽלְנוּ

   c) קָטַל קָֽטְלָה קָטַלְתָּ קָטַלְתְּ קָטַלְתִּי קָֽטְלוּ קְטַלְתֶּם קְטַלְתֶּן קָטַֽלְנוּ

   d) קָטַל קָֽטְלָה קָטַלְתָּ קָטַלְתְּ קָטַלְתִּי קָֽטְלוּ קְטַלְתֶּם קְטַלְתֶּן קָטַֽלְנוּ

7. (T/F) The negative particle לֹא is always placed *after* the verb.

8. Translate: זָכַרְנוּ אֶת־הַתּוֹרָה

   a) I remembered the law

   b) They remembered the law

   c) We remembered with the law

   d) We remembered the law

9. Translate: וְהִנֵּה אָנֹכִי עִמָּךְ

    a) And behold, we are your people
    b) And behold, I am with you (2fs)
    c) And behold, I am with you (2ms)
    d) None of the above

10. Translate: כָּבֵד

    a) To be heavy
    b) Heavy
    c) Both A or B
    d) None of the above

CHAPTER 14

Qal Perfect Weak Verbs

You Should Know

- בּוֹא
  - (Q) to go in, enter, come to, come upon; (Hi) bring (in), come (in); (Hoph) be brought

- בָּנָה
  - (Q) to build (up), rebuild, build (establish) a family; (Ni) be built, have a child (by or from)

- יָלַד
  - (Q) to bear (children), give birth, bring forth, beget; (Ni) be born; (Pi) help at birth, serve as midwife; (Pu) be born; (Hi) become the father of, beget

- יָרֵא
  - (Q) to fear, be afraid, in awe of, reverence; (Ni) be feared, held in honor

- יָרַד
  - (Q) to go down, descend; (Hi) bring down, lead down

- לָקַח
  - (Q) to take, grasp, capture, seize; (Ni) be captured, taken away

- מוּת
  - (Q) to die; (Hi) kill, put to death; (Hoph) be killed

- נָפַל
  - (Q) to fall, fall upon; (Hi) cause to fall, bring to ruin

- נָשָׂא

  – (Q) to lift, carry, raise, bear (load or burden), take (away); (Ni) be carried, lifted up, exalted; (Pi) lift up, exalt; (Hith) lift oneself up, exalt oneself

- עָבַר

  – (Q) to pass over, pass through, pass by, cross; (Hi) cause to pass over, bring over, cause or allow to pass (through), cause to pass through fire, sacrifice

- Of first importance is the need to memorize the strong verb paradigm and the Perfect sufformatives (13.5). The Perfect sufformatives will not change, despite any weakness in the verbal root.

- Guttural consonants cannot take a Vocal Shewa and will prefer some type of a-vowel, usually Hateph Pathach. This accounts for changes in I-Guttural, II-Guttural, and doubly weak verbs.

- With III-א weak verbs, the א is quiescent. This causes the loss of the Daghesh Lene in the ת of the Perfect sufformatives because the ת is now preceded by a vowel.

- With III-ה weak verbs, the final ה of the verbal root is lost in all forms of the Qal Perfect paradigm. All second and first person forms of this paradigm, both singular and plural, have the diagnostic Hireq Yod stem vowel (בָּנִיתָ). Additionally, the Daghesh Lene that is expected in the ת of the Perfect sufformatives is lost because this begadkephat consonant is preceded by a vowel (the Hireq Yod stem vowel).

- With Geminate verbs like סָבַב (to go around), expect the assimilation of the first Geminate consonant into the second Geminate consonant with a resulting Daghesh Forte in all second and first person forms (סַבּוֹתָ). The Holem Waw (וֹ) connecting vowel is also a diagnostic feature of this weak verb class. As with III-א and III-ה verbs, the Daghesh Lene that is expected in the ת of the Perfect sufformatives is lost because the ת is preceded by a vowel.

- With strong Biconsonantal verbs, *all third person forms* have Qamets under the first root consonant, while all other forms (second and first person) have Pathach.

Quiz

1. (T/F) Guttural consonants cannot take a Vocal Shewa and will prefer some type of e-vowel, usually Hateph Seghol.

2. What motivates the loss of the Daghesh Lene in the ת of the Perfect sufformatives of III-א verbs.

   a) Shewa is no longer under the third consonant
   b) The quiescing of the א
   c) The ת is preceded by a vowel sound
   d) All of the above

3. (T/F) III-ה verbs were originally III-י verbs.

4. Which diagnostic feature is unique to the identification of a Qal Perfect Geminate verb?

   a) A hireq yod (י) connecting vowel
   b) The loss of the Daghesh Lene in the Taw (ת)
   c) A Holem Waw connecting vowel (ו)
   d) None of the above

5. (T/F) The lexical form of a Biconsonantal verb is the Qal Perfect 3ms form.

6. Weak Biconsonantal verbs have which vowel under the first root consonant?

   a) Tsere (בֵא)
   b) Qamets Hatuf (בֳא)
   c) Pathach (בַא)
   d) Qamets (בָא)

7. (T/F) Due to vocalization changes in the Qal Weak Verbs, the perfect sufformatives also change.

8. Translate: בָּנְתָה
   a) She built
   b) You (2ms) built
   c) You (2fs) built
   d) He built

9. Translate: רָאִיתָ
   a) You saw (2fs)
   b) You saw (2ms)
   c) I saw
   d) We saw

10. Translate: קָם
   a) He rose
   b) She rose
   c) I rose
   d) We rose

CHAPTER 15

Qal Imperfect Strong Verbs

You Should Know

- חָיָה
  - (Q) to live, be alive, revive, restore to life; (Pi) preserve alive, let live, give life; (Hi) preserve, keep alive, revive, restore to life

- יָכֹל
  - (Q) to be able, capable of, endure, prevail

- כָּרַת
  - (Q) to cut, cut off, cut down; (idiom) to make a covenant (with בְּרִית); (Ni) be cut off (down); (Hi) cut off, destroy, exterminate

- סוּר
  - (Q) to turn (aside), turn off, leave (off), desist; (Hi) remove, take away, get rid of

- עָבַד
  - (Q) to work, serve, toil

- עָנָה
  - (Q) to answer, respond, reply, testify; (Ni) be answered

- אֹזֶן
  - ear

- אַיִל
  - ram, ruler; (adj) mighty

- זֶבַח
  - sacrifice

- חַיִּים
  - life, lifetime

- The Qal stem is used to express *simple action* with an *active voice*. The Imperfect conjugation is used to express an *incomplete action*, which may be translated with either the English present or future tense.

- The Imperfect conjugation is also called the *prefix* conjugation because every form takes a verbal prefix called a *preformative*. The preformatives are unique to the Imperfect conjugation in the Qal and derived stems.

- With the Imperfect inflection of stative verbs, the stem vowel is Pathach and not Holem.

- Imperfect verbs are negated with the particles אַל and לֹא. The negative particle לֹא may be used before an Imperfect verb to express an absolute or permanent prohibition. The negative particle אַל before an Imperfect is used to express an immediate and specific prohibition.

- It is important to understand that the use of the Imperfect (prefix) conjugation described in this section (15.2) represents only one of several possible uses. Additional uses of the Imperfect conjugation are described in section 17 and 23.

Quiz

1. What is the Imperfect conjugation used to express? (Choose the *best* answer.)

    a) Future tense
    b) Present tense
    c) Completed action
    d) Incomplete action

2. What is another name for the Imperfect conjugation?

   a) Preformative conjugation

   b) Prefix conjugation

   c) Sufformative conjugation

   d) Suffix conjugation

3. Correctly identify, in the order presented in *BBH*, the Qal Imperfect Paradigm of the Strong Verb.

   a) יִקְטֹל תִּקְטֹל תִּקְטֹל תִּקְטְלִי אֶקְטֹל יִקְטְלוּ תִּקְטֹלְנָה תִּקְטְלוּ תִּקְטֹלְנָה נִקְטֹל

   b) יִקְטֹל תִּקְטֹל תִּקְטֹל תִּקְטֹלְנָה תִּקְטְלוּ אֶקְטֹל יִקְטְלוּ תִּקְטֹלְנָה נִקְטֹל

   c) יִקְטֹל תִּקְטֹל תִּקְטֹל תִּקְטְלִי אֶקְטֹל יִקְטֹל תִּקְטְלוּ תִּקְטֹלְנָה תִּקְטֹלְנָה נִקְטֹל

   d) יִקְטֹל תִּקְטֹל תִּקְטֹל תִּקְטְלִי אֶקְטֹלְנָה תִּקְטֹלְנָה תִּקְטְלוּ יִקְטְלוּ אֶקְטֹל תִּקְטֹלְנַה נִקְטֹל

4. With some frequency, the 3mp and 2mp forms will be written with a final נ. What is this *Nun* called?

   a) Adversative Nun

   b) Consecutive Nun

   c) Nun Paragogicum

   d) Repetitive Nun

5. What are the *primary* diagnostic features of the Qal Imperfect Strong Verb (יִקְטֹל)?

   a) Hireq-Shewa-Holem stem vowel pattern

   b) Hireq-Shewa pattern

   c) *Yod* by itself

   d) Prefix-Hireq-Holem stem vowel pattern

6. What happens to the stem vowel of different stative verbs when inflected in the Imperfect?

   a) They take their class-corresponding stem vowel as they do in the Perfect

   b) They all take a tsere ( ) stem vowel regardless of class

c) They all take a pathach (ֲ) stem vowel regardless of class

d) They lose their stem vowel and get replaced with the diagnostic holem of the Imperfect

7. (T/F) The negative particle לֹא can express an immediate, specific, non-durative prohibition when preceding the Imperfect, while אַל can express an absolute or permanent prohibition.

8. Translate תִּזְכֹּרְנָה.

a) They will remember (3fp)

b) You remember (2fp)

c) You will remember (2fp)

d) All of the above

9. Choose the correct writing of the *stative* verb "to be heavy" in the 3fs.

a) תִּכְבֹּד

b) תִּכְבֵּד

c) תִּכְבַּד

d) תִּכְבַד

10. Translate: בַּסֵּפֶר (to write) אַל־תִּכְתֹּב

a) You (2ms) shall *never* write in the book!

b) She will not write in the book!

c) Do not write (2ms) in the book!

d) She will never write in the book!

CHAPTER 16

Qal Imperfect
Weak Verbs

You Should Know

- גָּאַל
  - (Q) to redeem, act as kinsman (perform the responsibilities of the next of kin), avenge

- חָטָא
  - (Q) to miss (a goal or mark), sin, commit a sin; (Pi) make a sin offering; (Hi) cause to sin

- יָסַף
  - (Q) to add, continue (to do something again); (Hi) add, increase, do again and again

- יָרַשׁ
  - (Q) to inherit, take possession of, dispossess, impoverish; (Hi) cause to possess or inherit, dispossess

- כָּפַר
  - (Pi) to cover (over), atone (for), make atonement

- נָטָה
  - (Q) to spread out, stretch out, extend, pitch (a tent), turn, bend; (Hi) turn, incline, stretch out, spread out

- עָזַב
  - (Q) to leave, leave behind, forsake, abandon, set free

- קָרַב
  - (Q) to approach, draw near, come near; (Hi) bring (near), present, offer a sacrifice or offering

- רָבָה
  - (Q) to be(come) numerous, great, increase; (Hi) make many, make great, multiply, increase

- שָׁתָה
  - (Q) to drink

- In this section you were not required to memorize any weak verb paradigms. Rather, you must study and understand the types of changes that occur in each of the various weak verb classes.

- There are four triconsonantal weak verb classes that appear with only two root letters when inflected in the Qal Imperfect. It is important to memorize those features that distinguish each weak verb class in order to properly reconstruct the verbal root for parsing and translation.

- I-י verbs drop their first root consonant but will be identifiable by the Tsere preformative vowel for Type 1 verbs. Type 2 verbs have the Hireq Yod preformative vowel. The verb הָלַךְ (to walk) also inflects like a I-י verb of the Type 1 class.

- I-נ verbs assimilate the נ of the first root consonant into the second root consonant. The resulting Daghesh Forte will enable you to identify the missing consonant as I-נ. The verb לָקַח (to take) also inflects like a I-נ verb with assimilation of the ל.

- III-ה verbs drop their final root consonant but are identifiable by their distinctive הֶ ending (in those forms without a sufformative).

- Geminate verbs retain only one Geminate consonant in the Imperfect conjugation. In some forms, this weak class is identifiable by a Daghesh Forte in the remaining Geminate consonant. In those forms without a Daghesh Forte, it is identifiable by a Qamets or Tsere preformative vowel in most forms.

Quiz

1. In the II-Guttural and III-ע/ח Imperfect weak verb category, what does the stem vowel shift to and why?

    a) Tsere (ֵ); Gutturals prefer e-type vowels

    b) Pathach (ַ); Gutturals prefer a-type vowels

    c) Tsere (ֵ); It's in a closed, accented syllable

    d) Pathach (ַ); It's in a closed, accented syllable

2. Which ending do III-ה verbs *without a sufformative* take?

    a) No ending

    b) ֶה

    c) ֵה

    d) י

3. Choose the correct pointing of Type 1 I-Guttural Imperfect verbs.

    a) יֶחֱזֹק

    b) יַחֲזֹק

    c) יֶחֲזֹק

    d) יֶחֱזַק

4. Parse: אֹמַר

    a) Qal Imperfect 3ms from אמר

    b) Qal Perfect 1cs from אמר

    c) Qal Imperfect 1cs from אמר

    d) Qal Perfect 3ms from אמר

5. (T/F) With Qal Imperfect Biconsonantal verbs, the medial vowel letter will reappear when inflected.

6. (T/F) With Qal Imperfect Biconsonantal verbs, the preformative vowel is Qamets (ָ) in *every* inflection.

7. What primary diagnostic should be recognized in order to reconstruct the root of a I-י verb?

    a) The Yod (י) from the root is retained

    b) A Pathach (ַ) under the preformative

    c) A Tsere (ֵ) under the preformative

    d) None of the above

8. Parse: תֵּלֵךְ

   a) Qal Imperfect 3fs or 2ms from ילד
   b) Qal Imperfect 2ms from הלך
   c) Qal Imperfect 3fs or 2ms from הלך
   d) Qal Imperfect 2ms from ילד

9. What is the *primary* diagnostic feature of the Qal Imperfect I-נ weak verb category?

   a) The Holem stem vowel in Type 1
   b) The Pathach stem vowel in Type 2
   c) The assimilated Nun as a Daghesh Lene in the second root consonant
   d) The assimilated Nun as a Daghesh Forte in the second root consonant

10. Which Hebrew verb can also inflect like a I-נ verb?

   a) הָלַךְ (To walk)
   b) יָלַד (To bear)
   c) לָקַח (To take)
   d) לָמַד (To learn)

CHAPTER 17

Waw Consecutive

You Should Know

- אָבַד
  - (Q) to perish, vanish, be(come) lost, go astray; (Pi) cause to perish, destroy; (Hi) exterminate

- אָהֵב
  - (Q) to love (of human and divine love); (Pi ptc) lover

- אָסַף
  - (Q) to gather (in), take in, take away, destroy; (Ni) be gathered, taken away, assemble

- גָּלָה
  - (Q) to uncover, reveal, disclose; (Ni) uncover, reveal oneself, be revealed, exposed; (Pi) uncover, reveal, disclose; (Hi) take (carry away) into exile

- טָהֵר
  - (Q) to be clean (ceremonially), pure (morally); (Pi) cleanse, purify, pronounce clean; (Hith) purify or cleanse oneself

- כָּלָה
  - (Q) to be complete, finished, at an end, accomplished, spent, exhausted, come to an end; (Pi) complete, finish, bring to an end

- רוּם
  - (Q) to be high, exalted, rise, arise; (Hi) raise, lift up, exalt, take away; (Hoph) be exalted; (Polel) exalt, bring up, extol, raise (children)

- שָׁפַט

  - (Q) to judge, make a judgment, decide (between), settle (a dispute or controversy); (Ni) go to court, plead, dispute

- אֹהֶל

  - tent

- אֱמֶת

  - truth, fidelity

- When an Imperfect verb is prefixed with Waw Consecutive, it will be translated with the values of a Perfect verb.

- The consecutive Imperfect is commonly translated with the English past tense (he killed) or present perfect tense (he has killed).

- With the prefixing of the Waw Consecutive, the spelling of the Imperfect verb remains the same. Be certain to note how these forms are translated.

- In most verb classes, the prefixing of the Waw Consecutive does not change the spelling of the Imperfect verb itself.

- When a Perfect verb is prefixed with Waw Consecutive, it will be translated with the values of the Imperfect.

- The consecutive Perfect is used for the future tense narrative sequence.

- Infrequently, the Perfect may appear with the regular conjunction and not with the Waw Consecutive. In these instances, the verbal construction is translated with "and" plus the past tense.

Quiz

1. (T/F) When an Imperfect is prefixed with a Waw Consecutive, it will be translated with the retention of its Imperfective form.

2. Identify the correct spelling diagnostics of the Imperfect with Waw Consecutive.

    a) וְיִקְטֹל

    b) וַיִּקְטֹל

    c) וַיִקְטֹל

    d) וִיִקְטֹל

3. Translate: וַיִּכְתֹּב

    a) And he wrote

    b) He writes

    c) And he will write

    d) He wrote

4. (T/F) The *consecutive Perfect* is used for the future tense narrative sequence.

5. (T/F) In the context of Hebrew narrative, the consecutive Imperfect is *normally* used for the *past tense narrative sequence*.

6. (T/F) When a *Perfect* verb is prefixed with the Waw Consecutive, it will be translated with the values of the *Imperfect*.

7. Identify the correct spelling diagnostics of the Perfect with the Waw Consecutive.

    a) וְקָטַל

    b) וְקֶטַל

    c) וַקְטֹל

    d) וִקָטַל

8. How would you distinguish a Perfect verb prefixed with the Waw Consecutive from a Conjunction Waw?

    a) *Only* context can determine

    b) In the 2ms and 1cs forms, the Waw Consecutive on the Perfect retains the accent on the second syllable whereas the Conjunction does not

    c) The Waw Conjunction will never change its form (וְ)

    d) In the 2ms and 1cs forms, the Waw Consecutive on the Perfect usually places the accent on the final syllable whereas the Conjunction does not

9. (T/F) Given the frequency of temporal modifiers such as וַיְהִי, it is preferable to translate the Waw Consecutive every time in the interest of good English style.

10. Parse: וְזָכַר

    a) Qal Imperfect 3ms from זכר with Waw Conjunction

    b) Qal Imperfect 3ms from זכר with Waw Consecutive

    c) Qal Perfect 3ms from זכר with Waw Conjunction (could also be Waw Consecutive, depends on context)

    d) Qal Perfect 3mp from זכר with Waw Consecutive

CHAPTER 18

Qal Imperative

You Should Know

- בָּחַר
  - (Q) to choose, test, examine

- בִּין
  - (Q) to understand, perceive, consider, give heed to; (Ni) be discerning, have understanding; (Hi) understand, teach; (Hith) show oneself perceptive

- דָּרַשׁ
  - (Q) to seek, inquire (of or about), investigate, require, demand

- הָרַג
  - (Q) to kill, slay

- חָפֵץ
  - (Q) to delight in, take pleasure in, desire, be willing

- קָדַשׁ
  - (Q) to be holy, set apart or consecrated; (Ni) be honored or treated as holy; (Pi) set apart, consecrate or dedicate as holy; (Hi) consecrate, dedicate or declare as holy; (Hith) show or keep oneself holy

- רָעָה
  - (Q) to pasture, tend (flocks), graze, shepherd, feed

- שָׁאַל
  - (Q) to ask (of), inquire (of), request, demand

- בַּעַל
  - owner, master, husband, (divine title) Baal

- שֵׁבֶט
  - rod, staff, scepter, tribe

- The Imperative is used primarily to express direct commands. It can also be used to grant permission or to communicate a request. The Hebrew Imperative *occurs only in the second person, singular and plural*.

- In the strong verb, the Qal Imperative forms are related to their corresponding Imperfect forms. Remove the Imperfect preformative from the four second person forms and you have the basic Imperative paradigm. Some variation in spelling does occur in certain weak verb classes.

- To produce a negative command, the Imperative is not negated. Prohibitions (negative commands) are expressed with the negative particles לֹא and אַל followed by the second person Imperfect.

- Imperatives may be followed by the particle נָא, which can be translated as "please" or simply left untranslated. This particle may be connected to the Imperative with Maqqef.

- There are several important sequences involving the Imperative conjugation, three of which include: (1) several Imperative verbs in succession that may be related consequentially or sequentially; (2) the Imperative followed by the second person consecutive Perfect to indicate consecution of imperatival force; and (3) an Imperative followed by an Imperfect, a construction that will create a purpose or result clause.

Quiz

1. (T/F) The Imperative conjugation is primarily used to express direct commands.

2. Correctly identify, in the order presented in *BBH*, the Qal Imperative Paradigm of the Strong Verb.

a) קְטֹל קִטְלִי קְטֹל קִטְלִי קִטְלוּ קְטֹלְנָה קִטְלוּ קְטֹלְנָה קְטֹל
b) קְטֹל קִטְלִי קִטְלוּ קְטֹלְנָה
c) קְטֹל קִטְלִי קִטְלוּ קְטֹלְנָה
d) קְטֹל קִטְלִי קְטֹל קִטְלִי קִטְלוּ קְטֹלְנָה קִטְלוּ קְטֹלְנָה קְטֹל

3. Identify the 2ms Imperative of שָׁמַר.

a) שְׁמֹר
b) שָׁמְרָה
c) שָׁמְרָה
d) Either A or B

4. What diagnostic ending can help you identify III-ה Imperative verbs in the 2ms?

a) הָ
b) הֶ
c) הֵ
d) וֹת

5. (T/F) In the strong verb, the Qal Imperative forms are related to their corresponding Imperfect forms.

6. What can help with the identification of the Imperative I-נ verb category?

a) The presence of the Nun
b) The absence of the Nun
c) The assimilated Daghesh Forte without the Imperfect Preformative
d) Either A or B

7. (T/F) Because the Imperative conjugation occurs exclusively in the third person, there are only four forms to study.

8. (T/F) The Imperative verbal form is like an Imperfect without the preformative.

9. Identify the 2ms Imperative of נפל

a) תִּפֹּל

b) נָפֹל

c) נִפַּלְנָה

d) נִפְלִי

10. Which particle is often used in conjunction with the imperatives, meaning "please" or left untranslated?

a) הֲ

b) נָה

c) נָא

d) יֵשׁ

CHAPTER 19

Pronominal Suffixes on Verbs

You Should Know

- בָּטַח
  - (Q) to trust, rely upon

- בָּכָה
  - (Q) to weep (in grief or joy), weep (for)

- לָבַשׁ
  - (Q) to put on a garment, clothe, be clothed; (Hi) clothe

- שָׂרַף
  - (Q) to burn (completely), destroy; (Ni) be burned

- שָׁלֵם
  - (Q) to be complete, finished; (Pi) complete, finish, make whole, restore, reward; (Hi) bring to completion, consummate

- דּוֹר
  - generation

- זֶרַע
  - seed, offspring, descendants

- חוּץ
  - outside, street

- מְלָאכָה
  - work, occupation, service

- עָוֹן

    - transgression, iniquity, guilt, punishment (of sin)

- The Pronominal Suffixes—The suffixes added to the definite direct object marker are the same suffixes that you will see on verbs. In general, verbs use Type 1 pronominal suffixes with an objective translation value.

- When a pronoun is the direct object of a verb, it may be attached to either the definite direct object marker or directly to the verb.

- In general, Perfect, Imperfect, and Imperative verbs use Type 1 pronominal suffixes with an objective translation value. With the Imperfect, three additional suffixes must be memorized. These are the so-called Nun-suffixes. You must be able to recognize and identify the person, gender, and number of all pronominal suffixes.

- You will need to become familiar with the spelling changes that occur in the verb stem with the addition of pronominal suffixes to the Perfect, Imperfect, and Imperative.

- The addition of certain pronominal suffixes to verbal forms that end in a consonant will frequently require some type of connecting vowel between the verbal stem and pronominal suffix. In general, Perfect verbs prefer a-class connecting vowels (Pathach or Qamets), whereas Imperfect and Imperative verbs prefer e-class connecting vowels (Seghol or Tsere).

Quiz

1. (T/F) When a pronoun is the direct object of a verb it can *only* be attached to the verb as a pronominal suffix.

2. Translate: קְטָלוֹהָ
    a) They killed
    b) They killed him
    c) She was killed
    d) They killed her

3. How would you correctly write, "They killed me?"

   a) קְטָלוּנִי
   b) קְטָלוּנִי
   c) קְטָלוּנִי
   d) קְטָלוּנִי

4. (T/F) Some suffixes are spelled differently, depending on whether they are added to a Perfect form that ends in a consonant or one that ends in a vowel.

5. The suffixes נָה ֶ/נּוּ/ךָ ֶ + accents are all examples of

   a) Type 1 suffixes
   b) Type 2 suffixes
   c) Nun-suffixes
   d) 3ms-suffixes

6. Which suffix could you attach to an Imperfect verb so its direct object is "him?"

   a) וֹ
   b) הוּ
   c) נּוּ ֶ
   d) All of the above

7. (T/F) When an Imperfect *strong* verb takes a pronominal suffix, the stem vowel will reduce from Holem to Shewa (יִקְטֹל ← יִקְטְל).

8. Parse: וַיִּתְּנֵם

   a) Qal Perfect 3ms from נתן + Waw Consecutive + 3fp suffix
   b) Qal Imperfect 3ms from נתן + Waw Consecutive + 3mp suffix
   c) Qal Perfect 3ms from נתן + Waw Consecutive + 3mp suffix
   d) Qal Imperfect 3ms from נתן + Waw Consecutive + 3fp suffix

9. What spelling change occurs in the Qal Imperative 2ms before a pronominal suffix?

   a) קְטֹל ← קָטְל
   b) קְטֹל ← קָטָל
   c) קְטֹל ← קְטָל
   d) קְטֹל ← קָטְל

10. Translate: שְׁפָטֵנִי

   a) He judged me
   b) He will judge me
   c) Judge me!
   d) He shall judge me!

CHAPTER 20

Qal Infinitive Construct

You Should Know

- טָמֵא
  - (Q) to be(come) unclean; (Ni) defile oneself; (Pi) defile, pronounce or declare unclean; (Hith) defile oneself, become unclean

- נָגַע
  - (Q) to touch, strike, reach; (Hi) touch, reach, throw, arrive

- נוּס
  - (Q) to flee, escape

- סָבַב
  - (Q) to turn (about), go around, surround; (Ni) turn; (Hi) cause to go around, lead around

- סָפַר
  - (Q) to count; (Pi) count, recount, make known, proclaim, report, tell

- קָרָא
  - (Q) to meet, encounter, happen

- שָׂמַח
  - (Q) to rejoice, be joyful, glad; (Pi) cause to rejoice, gladden, make someone happy

- שָׁבַר
  - (Q) to break (up), break in pieces, smash, shatter; (Ni) be smashed, broken, shattered or destroyed; (Pi) shatter, smash, break

- לִקְרַאת
  - toward, against, opposite

- בְּקֶרֶב
  - in the middle of, among

- The Infinitive Construct is not inflected for person, gender, or number. In all strong and many weak verbal roots, its basic form is identical to the Qal Imperative 2ms.

- Three weak verb classes (III-ה, I-נ, and I-י) have Infinitive Construct forms that vary significantly from the vowel pattern of the strong verb.

- The Infinitive Construct may occur with prepositional prefixes, pronominal suffixes, or both.

- The Infinitive Construct may occur with a pronominal suffix that can function as either the subject or object of the verbal idea.

- The Infinitive Construct is negated with בְּלְתִּי or לְבִלְתִּי ("not" or "in order not").

Quiz

1. Infinitives are
   a) Verbal adjectives
   b) Continuous verbs
   c) Verbal nouns
   d) Either B or C

2. (T/F) The Infinitive Construct is *not* inflected for person, gender, or number.

3. Correctly identify the Infinitive Construct Strong verb form.
   a) קְטֵל
   b) קָטַל
   c) קָטֵל
   d) קְטֹל

4. (T/F) בְּחֹר: Qal Infinitive Construct from בחר *or* Qal Imperative 2ms from בחר

5. The Infinitive Construct form of III-ה verbs ends in

    a) ה֔

    b) ה֖

    c) וֹת

    d) ה֔

6. How do you recognize I-נ verbs in the Infinitive Construct?

    a) The Nun is sometimes retained

    b) The Shewa-Holem diagnostic

    c) Some forms will drop the Nun and add a diagnostic ת at the end

    d) All of the above

7. (T/F) When the Infinitive Construct takes a pronominal suffix, the Pronoun can act *only* as the direct object.

8. What can be expressed by prefixing the preposition לְ to an Infinitive Construct?

    a) Purpose, Intention, or Result

    b) A Verbal Noun

    c) Complementary Action

    d) All of the above

9. What can be expressed by prefixing the preposition בְּ or כְּ to an Infinitive Construct?

    a) A Verbal Noun

    b) An Inceptive

    c) A Temporal Clause

    d) All of the above

10. How is the Infinitive Construct negated?

    a) לֹא

    b) אַל

    c) בִּלְתִּי

    d) Infinitive Constructs cannot be negated

ANSWER KEY

1. C, 2. T, 3. D, 4. F, 5. C, 6. D, 7. F, 8. D, 9. C, 10. C

CHAPTER 21

Qal Infinitive Absolute

You Should Know

- זָבַח
  - (Q) to slaughter (for sacrifice), sacrifice; (Pi) offer sacrifice, sacrifice

- חָנָה
  - (Q) to decline, camp, encamp, pitch camp, lay siege to

- נָחָה
  - (Q) to rest, settle down, repose; (Hi) cause to rest, secure rest, set, leave (behind or untouched)

- נָסַע
  - (Q) to pull (out or up), set out, start out, depart, journey

- פָּנָה
  - (Q) to turn (toward, from, to the side, away)

- פָּתַח
  - (Q) to open (up); (Ni) be opened, loosened, set free; (Pi) let loose, loosen

- רָדַף
  - (Q) to pursue, follow after, chase, persecute

- שָׂנֵא
  - (Q) to hate; (Pi ptc) enemy

- שָׁאַר
  - (Ni) to remain, be left over, survive; (Hi) leave (someone or something) remaining

- מוֹעֵד

  - appointed time (of feast), meeting place, assembly

- The Infinitive Absolute occurs less frequently than any other Hebrew conjugation, with only 817 total occurrences. Like the Infinitive Construct, the Infinitive Absolute is also a verbal noun. With regard to function, however, there is no precise English equivalent to the Hebrew Infinitive Absolute.

- The Infinitive Absolute is not inflected for person, gender, or number. There is, therefore, only one form to memorize. This form is easy to identify and varies little with weak verbal roots.

- The stem vowel of the Infinitive Absolute may be written as Holem Waw or defectively as Holem.

- Most weak verb forms follow the strong verb קָטוֹל or קָטֹל pattern. Remember, however, that III-ע/ח verbs have Furtive Pathach, III-ה verbs occur in one of two forms, and Bi-consonantal verbs have the Holem Waw or Holem vowel.

- The Infinitive Absolute is a verbal noun with a variety of uses. The four most common uses are: (1) emphatic; (2) imperatival; (3) simultaneous; and (4) complementary.

Quiz

1. Identify the correct form(s) of the Qal Infinitive Absolute Strong Verb.

   a) קָטֹל
   b) קָטוֹל
   c) קְטֹל
   d) Both A and B

2. (T/F) Like the Infinitive Construct, the Infinitive Absolute may take prepositional prefixes and pronominal suffixes.

3. Which of the following exhibits the correct spelling pattern for Infinitive Absolute III-ה verbs (עָשֹׂה)?

    a) עָשׂוֹ

    b) עָשֹׂה

    c) עָשָׂה

    d) Either A or B

4. Which medial vowel letter do all Biconsonantal verbs take in the Infinitive Absolute?

    a) וּ

    b) יָ

    c) וֹ

    d) הַ

5. Translate: זָכוֹר אֶת־הַיּוֹם הַזֶּה

    a) He will surely remember this day

    b) To remember this day

    c) He will surely remember that day

    d) Remember this day

6. What is/are the main use(s) of the Infinitive Absolute?

    a) Emphatic

    b) Imperatival

    c) Inceptive

    d) Both A and B

7. Identify the Particle of existence.

    a) נָה

    b) אֵין

    c) נָא

    d) יֵשׁ

8. Identify the Particle of non-existence.

    a) נָה

    b) אֵין

    c) נָא

    d) יֵשׁ

9. Translate: שָׁמוֹעַ תִּשְׁמְעוּ

    a) He will listen
    b) You (2ms) will surely listen
    c) You (2ms) will listen
    d) He will surely listen

10. (T/F) The Infinitive Absolute, in some cases, *can* be inflected for person, gender, and number.

CHAPTER 22

Qal Participle

You Should Know

- אָרַר
  - (Q) to curse

- בּוֹשׁ
  - (Q) to be ashamed; (Hi) put to shame

- גָּדַל
  - (Q) to grow up, be(come) great, become strong, wealthy or important; (Pi) bring up (children), make great, extol; (Hi) make great, magnify, do great things

- חָשַׁב
  - (Q) to think, consider, devise, plan, value, esteem, reckon; (Ni) be reckoned, accounted, considere (as); (Pi) think, consider, devise, plan

- יָטַב
  - (Q) to be well with, go well with, be pleasing (to); (Hi) make things go well for, do good to, deal well with, treat kindly

- לָכַד
  - (Q) to take, capture, catch, seize; (Ni) be caught, captured

- נָגַשׁ
  - (Q) to draw near, come near, approach

- קָבַץ
  - (Q) to collect, gather, assemble (Ni) be gathered, assembled; (Pi) gather together, assemble

- קָבַר
  - (Q) to bury; (Ni) be buried

- שָׁכֵן
  - (Q) to settle (down), abide, reside, dwell, inhabit; (Pi) abide, dwell

- Participles are verbal adjectives. Like a verb, Participles have stem (Qal) and voice (active or passive) and may take a direct object. Like an adjective, they have gender and number. Participles do not have person.

- The Qal active Participle paradigm for the strong verb must be memorized. The inflectional endings are the same as those that you have memorized for adjectives and nouns.

- A Holem following the first root letter is diagnostic of the Qal *active* Participle.

- The only class of Qal active Participles without the Holem vowel is the Biconsonantal weak verb class (22.4.5). These weak verbs have a Qamets throughout.

- The Qal passive Participle paradigm for the strong verb must be memorized. The inflectional endings are the same as those you have memorized for adjectives and nouns.

- The three uses of the Participle (active and passive) are attributive, predicative, and substantive.

Quiz

1. Participles are
   a) Verbal nouns
   b) Verbal adjectives
   c) Verbal adverbs
   d) Verbal modifiers

2. (T/F) Participles can be inflected for person, gender, and number.

3. Which represents the correctly written form of the Qal Active Participle Strong Verb?

- a) קְטֵל
- b) קְטֹל
- c) קְטוֹל
- d) קֹטֵל

4. Which inflectional ending of the Qal Active Participle differs from that of other nouns and adjectives?

- a) The masculine plural (סִי)
- b) The feminine singular (ת ֶ)
- c) The feminine plural (וֹת)
- d) The feminine singular (ָה)

5. What is the III-ה ending on participles?

- a) הָ
- b) הֶ
- c) וֹת
- d) הֵ

6. Parse: קָמָה

- a) Qal Perfect 3fs from קוּם
- b) Qal Active Participle fp from קוּם
- c) Qal Active Participle fs from קוּם
- d) Qal Passive Participle fs from קוּם

7. Identify the correct spelling pattern for the Qal Passive Participle.

- a) קָטוּל
- b) קָטֵל
- c) קֹטֵל
- d) Both A and B

8. Which of the following correctly adds the Masculine Plural ending to the Qal Passive Participle?

- a) קְטוּלִים
- b) קְתוּלִים
- c) קְתוּלִים
- d) קְטוּלִים

9. In Qal Passive Participle III-ה verbs, the ה is replaced by what?

    a) A vowel letter (הֶ)

    b) A Taw (ת)

    c) A Yod (י)

    d) It will simply drop off

10. Identify how the Active Participle is being used in the following sentence:

וְהָיָה בֹעֵר (to burn) בָּאֵשׁ

    a) Attributively

    b) Predicatively

    c) Substantively

    d) None of the above

CHAPTER 23

Sentence Syntax

You Should Know

- בֶּגֶד
  - clothes, garment, covering

- בְּהֵמָה
  - animal(s), beast(s), cattle

- בְּכוֹר
  - firstborn, oldest offspring

- חָכְמָה
  - wisdom, skill

- חֵמָה
  - wrath, heat, poison

- חָצֵר
  - courtyard, village, settlement

- כֹּחַ
  - strength, power

- נְחֹשֶׁת
  - copper, bronze

- נָשִׂיא
  - chief, leader, prince

- עֶצֶם
  - bone, skeleton

- In Hebrew, word order for a verbal sentence is normally *verb-subject-object*. However, subjects and objects may appear before the verb in important contexts. Additionally, a verb may also be preceded by an adverb of time, an adverbial phrase, the word הִנֵּה (behold), an expression that provides circumstantial information, an independent personal pronoun, or a negative particle.

- When working with the Perfect and Imperfect conjugations, it is important to consider the position of the verb in its clause (first or non-first) and the use or non-use of the Waw Consecutive and the regular conjunction וְ.

- The regular Perfect does not normally appear first in its clause. The consecutive Perfect appears first in its clause. When following an Imperative verb, the consecutive Perfect may carry the full force of the preceding Imperative.

- The regular Imperfect does not normally appear first in its clause. The consecutive Imperfect appears first in its clause. The volitional Imperfect appears first in its clause but without the Waw Consecutive. When following an Imperative verb, the Imperfect (with the regular conjunction וְ) may create a purpose or result clause.

- In Hebrew, a verbless clause consists of a subject and a noun or its equivalent serving as the predicate. The subject and the predicate appear together (side by side) and may consist of a noun, adjective, independent personal pronoun, demonstrative pronoun, interrogative pronoun, prepositional phrase, or participle.

Quiz

1. What can offset a verb in a standard Hebrew sentence (V-S-O)?
    a) An adverb (עַתָּה)
    b) A temporal clause (וְהָיָה or וַיְהִי)
    c) A negative particle (לֹא)
    d) All of the above

2. (T/F) The verb is normally immediately followed by its subject if one is explicit.

3. What can help identify the Indirect Object (Dative) of a sentence in Hebrew?
   a) נָא
   b) אֶל־
   c) בְּ
   d) Both A and B

4. (T/F) In Hebrew, an Object can *never* precede its verb.

5. What happens when a Consecutive Perfect verb is preceded by an Imperative?
   a) The Perfect is translated in the future tense
   b) The Perfect is translated in the past tense
   c) The Perfect carries the full force of the Imperative
   d) The Perfect is translated as an Infinitive

6. (T/F) In Hebrew, the word order for a verbless clause is variable, but this variation is often insignificant.

7. Translate the following verbless clause: זֹאת הַבְּרִית
   a) This is the covenant
   b) This covenant
   c) Is this the covenant?
   d) This will be a covenant (to them)

8. (T/F) When an Imperfect verb is prefixed with the Waw Consecutive, it is normally translated as a future tense in English.

9. (T/F) When a Perfect verb is prefixed with the Waw Consecutive, it will be translated with the values of the Imperfect.

10. (T/F) If several Imperatives are strung together, they *must* use the Conjunction Waw to do this.

- נָכָה
  - (Hi) to strike, smite, beat, strike dead, destroy; (Hoph) be struck down dead, beaten

- נָצַב
  - (Ni) to stand (firm), take one's stand, station oneself, be positioned; (Hi) station, set (up), place, establish

- נָצַל
  - (Ni) to be rescued, delivered, saved; (Hi) tear from, take away, deliver from

- The Niphal stem is used to express *simple action* with either a *passive* or *reflexive* voice. It may also express a *reciprocal* type of action or the active voice of the Qal stem.

- Some verbs in the Niphal stem are translated with an active voice just like the Qal stem. This is frequently the case with verbal roots that are common in the Niphal stem but are not attested (or rarely attested) in the Qal stem.

- In the Niphal, the נ stem prefix is added to every form of every conjugation. In the Perfect, Participle, and one form of the Infinitive Absolute (נִקְטוֹל), the נ appears as a consonant in the spelling.

- In the Imperfect, Imperative, Infinitive Construct, and the other form of the Infinitive Absolute (הִקָּטוֹל), the נ assimilates into the first consonant of the verbal root and becomes a Daghesh Forte.

- It is not necessary that you memorize the paradigms in this section. Rather, you should memorize the diagnostic features of spelling for each conjugation.

Quiz

1. Identify the correct representation of the Niphal Perfect Strong Verb diagnostics.

  a) נְקְטָל
  b) נִקְטַל

CHAPTER 24

The Niphal Stem Strong Verbs

You Should Know

- אָמַן
  - (Ni) to be reliable, faithful or trustworthy; (Hi) believe (in), trust, have trust in, put trust in

- יָשַׁע
  - (Ni) to be delivered, victorious, receive help; (Hi) help, save, deliver, rescue, come to the aid of

- יָתַר
  - (Ni) to be left over, remain; (Hi) have (something) left over or remaining

- כּוּן
  - (Ni) to be established, steadfast, ready, arranged, stand firm; (Hi) establish, set up, prepare, make ready, make firm

- לָחַם
  - (Q, Ni) to fight, do battle with (rare in Q)

- מָלַט
  - (Ni) to escape, flee to safety, slip away; (Pi) let someone escape, save someone, leave undisturbed

- נָחַם
  - (Ni) to be sorry, regret, have compassion (on or for); (Pi) comfort, console

    c) נִקְטַל
    d) נִקְטָל

2. What kind of *action* does the Niphal express?

    a) Simple
    b) Intensive
    c) Causative
    d) Both A and C

3. Parse: נִקְטָל

    a) Niphal Imperfect 1cp from קטל
    b) Niphal Infinitive Absolute from קטל
    c) Niphal Imperfect 3ms from קטל
    d) Qal Imperfect 2mp from קטל

4. (T/F) The Niphal Stem expresses a passive voice only.

5. Which conjugations can be identified from the *He-Hireq-Qamets-Daghesh Forte* pattern in the Niphal (הִקָּטֵל)?

    a) Niphal Imperative
    b) Niphal Infinitive Construct
    c) Niphal Infinitive Absolute
    d) Both A and B

6. Parse: נִשְׁמַרְתֶּם

    a) Niphal Perfect 2fp from שמר
    b) Qal Perfect 2mp from נשם
    c) Niphal Perfect 2mp from נשם
    d) Niphal Perfect 2mp from שמר

7. Translate: הַנְּבִיאִים יִזָּכְרוּ

    a) The prophets were remembered
    b) The prophets will be remembered
    c) The prophets remembered
    d) Remember (2ms) the prophets

8. Identify the correct representation of the Niphal Infinitive Absolute diagnostics.

a) נִקְטוֹל

b) הִקָּטוֹל

c) נִקְטַל

d) Both A and B

9. Identify the correct representation of the Niphal Participle Strong Verb diagnostics.

a) נִקְטָל

b) נִקְטָל

c) נִקְטָל

d) נִקְטָל

10. Translate: נִזְכְּרוּ הַנְּבִיאִים

a) The prophets were remembered

b) The prophets will be remembered

c) The prophets remembered

d) Remember (2ms) the prophets

CHAPTER 25

The Niphal Stem Weak Verbs

You Should Know

- הָפַךְ
  - (Q) to turn, overturn, overthrow, destroy; (Ni) be destroyed, turned into, changed

- חָרָה
  - (Q) to be(come) hot, burn with anger, become angry

- רָעַע
  - (Q) to be bad, evil or displeasing; (Hi) do evil, do wickedly, do injury, harm, treat badly

- שָׂבַע
  - (Q) to be satisfied, have one's fill (of), eat or drink one's fill; (Hi) satisfy

- שָׁכַח
  - (Q) to forget; (Ni) be forgotten

- שָׁמֵם
  - (Q) to be deserted, uninhabited; (Ni) be made uninhabited, desolate, deserted; (Hi) make deserted or desolate

- זָכָר
  - male, man

- חֹשֶׁךְ
  - darkness

- כְּסִיל

  – fool, shameless person

- מִגְרָשׁ

  – open land, pasture

- Most of the diagnostics for the Niphal strong verb are retained in the III-א Niphal forms. The diagnostics are identical in the Imperfect, Imperative, Infinitive Construct, and Infinitive Absolute. The diagnostics of the Perfect and Participle exhibit only minor changes.

- The Niphal strong verb diagnostics are retained in the Imperfect, Imperative, Infinitive Construct, and Infinitive Absolute forms of III-ה verbs. With the Perfect and Participle, only the stem vowels of the strong verb are affected in this weak verb class.

- The changes that occur in the Niphal forms of I-Guttural verbal roots, while appearing drastic at first, are explained by rules that you have already learned.

- There are several other weak verb classes that are attested in the Niphal stem. The diagnostics of III-ע/ח weak verbs are identical to the strong verb. Biconsonantal, Geminate, and various doubly weak forms occur infrequently and do not warrant attention here.

- Mastery of the diagnostics for the strong and weak verbs already presented should be sufficient to enable you to successfully identify these more infrequent weak forms of the Niphal stem.

Quiz

1. (T/F) All conjugations of III-ה verbs change in the Niphal.

2. In the Niphal Perfect, why is the final ה of בָּנָה replaced by Tsere Yod in the 2ms form נִבְנֵיתָ?

   a) It is a diagnostic ending of verbs in the Perfect
   b) Closed accented syllables prefer a long vowel
   c) III-ה verbs used to be III-י
   d) Both A and C

3. Parse: יֵעָזֵב

   a) Niphal Imperfect 3ms from עזב

   b) Qal Imperfect 3ms from יעז

   c) Niphal Imperfect 3cp from עזב

   d) Qal Imperfect 2mp from עזב

4. What has happened to the initial נ of the root in the Niphal Perfect 1cs verb נִצַּלְתִּי?

   a) It has assimilated into the second root consonant as a Daghesh Lene

   b) It has assimilated into the second root consonant as a Daghesh Forte

   c) It has simply dropped off

   d) Nothing has happened to it, it remains the first root letter

5. In the Niphal stem, what happens to the נ when it tries to assimilate into a I-Guttural verb like נֶעֱזַב?

   a) It gets rejected resulting in the Type 1 vowel pattern for verbs with Gutturals

   b) It gets rejected and results in *compensatory* lengthening

   c) It gets rejected and results in *virtual doubling*

   d) Both A and B

6. (T/F) I-ו verbs were originally I-י.

7. What is the first root letter of the Niphal Imperfect 3ms verb יִוָּשֵׁב?

   a) Shureq

   b) Yod

   c) Waw with Daghesh Forte

   d) Waw with Daghesh Lene

8. Translate: עָרִים גְּדוֹלוֹת בָּאָרֶץ נִבְנוּ

   a) We built great cities in the land

   b) They built great cities in the land

   c) We will build great cities in the land

   d) Great cities were built in the land

9. Parse: הִוָּדְעִי

a) Niphal Imperative 2fs from וְדַע
b) Niphal Imperative 2fs from יָדַע
c) Niphal Imperfect 2ms from יָדַע
d) Niphal Imperfect 2fs from וְדַע

10. Parse: נוֹשֶׁבֶת

a) Niphal Partciple fs from יָשַׁב
b) Niphal Perfect 2fs from יָשַׁב
c) Niphal Participle fs from וְשַׁב
d) Niphal Perfect 2fs from וְשַׁב

CHAPTER 26

The Hiphil Stem
Strong Verbs

You Should Know

- בָּקַשׁ
  - (Pi) to seek, search for, look for, discover, demand, require;
    (Pu) be sought

- דָּבַר
  - (Q) to speak (rare in Q); (Pi) speak

- הָלַל
  - (Pi) to praise, sing hallelujah; (Pu) be praised, praiseworthy;
    (Hith) boast

- כָּסָה
  - (Q) to cover, conceal, hide; (Pi) cover (up), conceal, clothe

- מָהַר
  - (Pi) to hasten, hurry, go or come quickly

- נָבָא
  - (Ni) to prophesy, be in a state of prophetic ecstasy; (Hith)
    speak or behave as a prophet

- סָגַר
  - (Q) to shut (in), close; (Hi) deliver (up), hand over, surrender,
    give up

- צָוָה
  - (Pi) to command, give an order, charge; (Pu) be ordered, be
    told, receive a command

- קָטַר
  - (Pi) to make a sacrifice go up in smoke, offer (a sacrifice) by burning; (Hi) cause a sacrifice to go up in smoke

- שִׁיר
  - (Q) to sing (of); (Q ptc) singer

- The Hiphil stem may be used to express *causative* action with an *active* voice.

- The key words "cause" and "make" may be used to change the simple action of the Qal into the causative action of the Hiphil. Oftentimes, however, the more idiomatic translations are to be preferred.

- In addition to causative action, the Hiphil stem may also be used for *declarative* and *factitive* types of action, as well as the *simple* action of the Qal stem.

- There are a few other categories of verbal meaning in the Hiphil stem, such as denominative and permissive, but these are infrequent. Additionally, the meaning of some Hiphil verbs cannot be easily categorized. In such cases, you will need to check the lexicon in order to determine meaning.

- The most important diagnostic features of the Hiphil stem include: 1) ה prefix in all conjugations except the Imperfect and Participle; 2) Pathach under all preformatives and prefixes, except in the Perfect where it is Hireq; 3) Hireq Yod or Tsere stem vowel in all forms, except in the second and first person forms of the Perfect, where it is Pathach.

Quiz

1. Identify the correct form(s) of the Hiphil Perfect Strong Verb.
   - a) הִקְטֵל
   - b) הִקְטִיל
   - c) הִקְטַלְתָּ
   - d) Both B and C

2. Parse: הָקְטֵל

    a) Hiphil Perfect 3ms from קטל

    b) Niphal Infinitive Construct from קטל

    c) Niphal Imperative 2fs from קטל

    d) Hiphil Infinitive Construct from קטל

3. (T/F) The Hiphil stem is used to express a causative type of action with an active voice.

4. Identify the correct diagnostic representation of the Hiphil Imperfect Strong Verb.

    a) יְקְטִיל

    b) יָקְטֵל

    c) יֶקְטִיל

    d) יַקְטִיל

5. What are the four *main* uses of the Hiphil Stem?

    a) Causative, Simple, Declarative, Denominative

    b) Causative, Simple, Passive, Factitive

    c) Causative, Simple, Declarative, Factitive

    d) Causative, Reciprocal, Declarative, Factitive

6. Identify the correct diagnostic representation(s) of the Hiphil Imperative Strong Verb.

    a) הַקְטֵל

    b) הַקְטִילִי

    c) הַקְטֵלְנָה

    d) All of the above

7. Identify the correct diagnostic representation of the Hiphil Infinitive Construct Strong Verb.

    a) הַקְטֵל

    b) הַקְטִיל

    c) מַקְטִיל

    d) הִקְטִיל

8. Identify the correct diagnostic representation of the Hiphil Infinitive Absolute Strong Verb.

a) הַקְטֵל
b) הַקְטִיל
c) מַקְטִיל
d) הִקְטִיל

9. Identify the correct diagnostic representation of the Hiphil Participle Strong Verb.

a) הַקְטֵל
b) הַקְטִיל
c) מַקְטִיל
d) הִקְטִיל

10. Parse: לְהַגְדִּיל

a) Hiphil Infinitive Construct from גדל
b) Niphal Infinitive Construct from גדל
c) Hiphil Infinitive Construct from גדל with לְ preposition
d) Niphal Infinitive Construct from גדל with לְ preposition

CHAPTER 27

The Hiphil Stem Weak Verbs

You Should Know

- גּוּר
    - (Q) to sojourn, dwell (stay) as a foreigner or alien

- יָעַץ
    - (Q) to advise, counsel, plan, decide; (Ni) consult or take counsel together

- לָמַד
    - (Q) to learn; (Pi) teach

- מָכַר
    - (Q) to sell, hand over; (Ni) be sold, sell oneself (into slavery)

- מָשַׁל
    - (Q) to rule, reign, govern, have dominion

- עָזַר
    - (Q) to help, assist, come to the aid of

- קָלַל
    - (Q) to be small, insignificant, of little account, swift; (Ni, Pi) declare cursed; (Hi) treat with contempt

- קָנָה
    - (Q) to get, acquire, buy

- שָׁחַט
    - (Q) to slaughter (animals for sacrifice)

- כָּנָף
  - wing, edge, extremity

- In every conjugation except the Perfect the strong verb diagnostics of the Hiphil stem are preserved in this weak verb class.

- While it is not diagnostic, it is helpful to note that the guttural consonant in first root position takes a reduced vowel in every form of every conjugation, Hateph Seghol in the Perfect and Hateph Pathach in all other conjugations.

- Most of the Hiphil strong verb diagnostics are preserved in this weak verb class. The only variations are in the stem vowel of a few forms.

- Most of the Hiphil strong verb diagnostics are preserved in this weak verb class. All prefix and preformative consonants and vowels follow the pattern of the Hiphil strong verb. The stem vowel variations that do occur should be familiar to you as changes characteristic of the III-א weak verb class.

- In Hiphil III-ה verbs, all prefix and preformative consonants and vowels retain the strong verb diagnostics. Variation from the strong verb diagnostics occurs mainly in the stem vowels of the various conjugations. In most instances, however, the distinctive preformatives and prefixes should be sufficient for identifying Hiphil III-ה verbs.

- Note the III-ה diagnostic endings. These are the same endings that appear on all III-ה verbs in the Qal and derived stems. It will be helpful to review 25.5.3 and especially the chart entitled "Diagnostic Endings for III-ה Verbs in All Stems."

Quiz

1. הֶעֱמִיד: What has motivated the Seghol prefix vowel instead of the Hireq of the Strong Verb in this Hiphil Weak Verb?
   a) Compensatory Lengthening
   b) Virtual Doubling

    c) I-Guttural Verbs prefer a certain vowel pattern

    d) Propretonic reduction

2. Parse: תַּעֲמִידוּ

    a) Hiphil Perfect 3cp from עמד

    b) Hiphil Perfect 1cp from עמד

    c) Hiphil Imperfect 3mp from עמד

    d) Hiphil Imperfect 2mp from עמד

3. יַגְלֶה: What has happened to the expected *Hireq Yod* stem vowel that is diagnostic of the Hiphil Stem in this III-ה Hiphil verb?

    a) It simply dropped out

    b) Open tonic syllables prefer a long vowel

    c) III-ה verbs have their own stem vowels that replace whatever precedes them

    d) None of the above

4. Parse: וַיַּשְׁלֵךְ

    a) Hiphil Imperfect 3ms from שלך with Waw Conjunction

    b) Qal Imperfect 3ms from שלך with Waw Consecutive

    c) Piel Imperfect 3ms from שלך with Waw Consecutive

    d) Hiphil Imperfect 3ms from שלך with Waw Consecutive

5. הַצֵּל: What aids in the indication of this verb as a I-נ Hiphil Imperative?

    a) The Pathach Preformative

    b) The Daghesh Forte in the second root consonant

    c) The Tsere stem vowel

    d) All of the above

6. Parse: תּוֹדַעְנָה

    a) Hiphil Imperfect 3fp from ידע

    b) Hiphil Imperfect 2fp from ידע

    c) Hiphil Imperfect 3fp from ודע

    d) Either A or B

7. (T/F) In the Hiphil, every class of Biconsonantal verbs will exhibit *Hireq Yod* as the medial vowel letter.

8. What aids in the identification of Hiphil Biconsonantals in the Imperative, Infinitive Construct, and Infinitive Absolute?

  a) Qamets preformative vowel
  b) Tsere stem vowel
  c) Hireq Yod stem vowel
  d) All of the above

9. Parse: הִבְטִיחוּ

  a) Hiphil Perfect 3cp from בטח
  b) Niphal Imperfect 1cs from הבט with 3ms suffix
  c) Hiphil Perfect 1cp from בטח
  d) Niphal Infinitive Construct mp from בטח with 3ms suffix

10. What do the Piel, Pual, Hophal, and Hiphil Participles have in common?

  a) A Daghesh Forte in the second root consonant
  b) A Vocal Shewa under the preformative
  c) A מ prefix
  d) All of the above

CHAPTER 28

The Hophal Stem
Strong Verbs

You Should Know

- אָסַר
  - (Q) to tie, bind, fetter, imprison

- זָעַק
  - (Q) to cry (out), call for help, summon

- חָלָה
  - (Q) to be(come) weak, tired, sick; (Ni) be exhausted; (Pi) appease, flatter

- חָנַן
  - (Q) to be gracious to, show favor to, favor; (Hith) plead for grace, favor or compassion

- מָאַס
  - (Q) to refuse, reject, despise

- עוּר
  - (Q) to be awake, stir up; (Hi) arouse, rouse, wake up, stir up; (Polel) arouse, disturb, awaken

- עָרַד
  - (Q) to set in order, lay out, set in rows, arrange, stack (wood), draw up a battle formation

- רָחַץ
  - (Q) to wash (with water), wash (off or away), bathe, bathe oneself

- יָמִין
  - right hand, south

- מַרְאֶה
  - vision, sight, appearance

- The Hophal stem is used to express *causative* action with a *passive* voice. In most of its occurrences, the Hophal is the passive of the Hiphil.

- The Hophal conjugations are distinguished from other derived stem conjugations by their prefix or preformative vowels, Qibbuts or Qamets Hatuf. It is perhaps best to think of the Hophal prefix vowels in terms of vowel class rather than particular vowels.

- You should learn that the Hophal prefix vowel is variable between u-class and o-class vowels. With u-class vowels, Qibbuts appears most frequently, but Shureq also occurs in many weak verbs.

- With o-class vowels, Qamets Hatuf occurs most frequently, but Holem and Holem Waw also appear. Thinking of the Hophal prefix vowel in terms of vowel classes will prevent confusion when you encounter variation, especially in the weak verb forms.

- In the Perfect and Imperfect conjugations, the stem vowel is Pathach, except in those forms with sufformatives that begin with or consist of a vowel. In the Participle, the stem vowel is Qamets, except in the feminine singular.

Quiz

1. Identify the correct diagnostic pattern for the Hophal Strong Perfect.

   a) הָקְטַל

   b) הֻקְטַל

   c) הֳקְטַל

   d) Both B and C

2. The Hophal stem is used to express

    a) Intensive action with a passive voice

    b) Reflexive action with an active voice

    c) Causative action with a passive voice

    d) Causative action with an active voice

3. (T/F) Hophal Perfect 3ms form, הָקְטַל: The first vowel under the preformative is a Qamets Hatuf *because* it occurs in an *open* and *unaccented* syllable.

4. Identify the correct diagnostic pattern for the Hophal Strong Imperfect.

    a) יָקְטַל

    b) יְקַטֵּל

    c) יְקְטַל

    d) יָקְטֵל

5. Parse: הָשְׁלַכְתָּ

    a) Hophal Perfect 2ms from שׁלך

    b) Hiphil Perfect 2ms from שׁלך

    c) Niphal Infinitive Construct from שׁלך with 2fs suffix

    d) Hophal Perfect 2fs from שׁלך

6. Identify the correct diagnostic representation of the Hophal Participle Strong Verb.

    a) מָקְטִיל

    b) מָקְטָל

    c) מֻקְטָל

    d) Both B and C

7. (T/F) The Hophal Stem is not attested in the Infinitive Construct *or* the Infinitive Absolute.

8. Which stem includes a conjugation with a prefixed He exhibiting the diagnostic vowel pattern *Hireq-Qamets-Daghesh Forte*?

    a) Qal

    b) Niphal

    c) Hiphil

    d) Hophal

9. Which stem includes a conjugation with a prefixed He exhibiting a *Tsere* (_) stem vowel?

    a) Qal

    b) Niphal

    c) Hiphil

    d) Hophal

10. Parse: הָשְׁלַכְתָּ

    a) Hophal Perfect 2ms from שלך

    b) Hiphil Perfect 2ms from שלך

    c) Niphal Infinitive Construct from שלך with 2fs suffix

    d) Hophal Perfect 2fs from שלך

CHAPTER 29

The Hophal Stem
Weak Verbs

You Should Know

- גֵּר
  - stranger, sojourner, alien

- חַיָּה
  - animal, beast, living thing

- חֵלֶב
  - fat; (metaphorically) best, choice part

- חֲמוֹר
  - donkey

- יֶתֶר
  - rest, remainder, excess

- נַחַל
  - stream, brook, wadi

- עוֹר
  - skin, hide, leather

- עֹז
  - strength, power, might

- פֶּשַׁע
  - transgression, rebellion

- קָצֶה

  - end, border, outskirts

- Five weak verb classes preserve only two root consonants in the Hophal stem. With III-ה verbs, the final ה is lost.

- With I-נ verbs, the נ assimilates into the second root consonant and remains as a Daghesh Forte.

- With I-י verbs (originally I-ו), the vowel letter Shureq replaces the י as the prefix or preformative vowel in the Perfect, Imperfect, and Participle.

- With Geminate verbs, only one Geminate consonant is preserved, though it is represented as a Daghesh Forte in some forms.

- With Biconsonantal verbs, both root consonants remain and the prefix or preformative vowel is Shureq in every form of the Perfect, Imperfect, and Participle.

Quiz

1. (T/F) I-Guttural verbs in the Hophal prefer the Qibbuts (u-class) Preformative vowel.

2. Parse: הָעֳמַד
   - a) Hophal Perfect 2ms from עמד
   - b) Hophal Perfect 3ms from עמד
   - c) Hiphil Perfect 2ms from עמד
   - d) Hiphil Perfect 3ms from עמד

3. (T/F) III-ה verbs in the Hophal prefer the Qibbuts (u-class) Preformative vowel.

4. Parse: וַיַּעֲמֵד
   - a) Hiphil Imperfect 3ms from עמד
   - b) Hiphil Imperfect 3ms from עמד with Waw Consecutive
   - c) Hophal Imperfect 3ms from עמד with Waw Conjunction
   - d) Hiphil Imperfect 3ms from עמד with Waw Conjunction

5. (T/F) I-נ verbs in the Hophal prefer the Qibbuts (u-class) Preformative vowel

6. מֻצָּל: How would it be explained that this Hophal Participle is a I-נ verb?

    a) The Nun has dropped out because it preceded a guttural

    b) The Nun cannot be written as the first root consonant in the Hophal stem

    c) This is not a I-נ verb because the verbal root is מצל

    d) The Nun is weak and has assimilated into the צ as a Daghesh Forte

7. Parse: הוֹדִיע

    a) Hiphil Perfect 3ms from ידע

    b) Hiphil Infinitive Construct from ידע

    c) Hophal Perfect 3ms from ידע

    d) Either A or B

8. תּוֹדַעְנֶה: What changes would be necessary to make this I-י Hiphil Imperfect 2fp/3fp verbal form a Hophal?

    a) A Qibbuts under the Waw

    b) A Qamets stem vowel

    c) A Shureq (u-class vowel) after the Preformative

    d) A Qamets Hatuf stem vowel

9. (T/F) In Hophal Biconsonantal verbs, the medial vowel letters do not appear and usually take an a-class stem vowel (such as הוּקַם).

10. הוּסַבּוֹתָ: What aids in the identification of this verb as *Hophal* and *Geminate*?

    a) The Holem Waw connecting vowel in the Perfect

    b) The Daghesh Forte in the second root letter

    c) The Shureq prefix vowel

    d) All of the above

ANSWER KEY

1. F, 2. B, 3. F, 4. B, 5. T, 6. D, 7. D, 8. C, 9. T, 10. D

CHAPTER 30

The Piel Stem
Strong Verbs

You Should Know

- חָלַל
  - (Ni) to be defiled, profaned, defile oneself; (Pi) profane, pollute, defile; (Hi) let something be profaned

- נָגַד
  - (Hi) to tell, announce, report, declare, inform; (Hoph) be told, announced, reported

- שָׁבַע
  - (Ni) to swear (take) an oath; (Hi) cause to take an oath, plead with someone

- שָׁלַךְ
  - (Hi) to send, throw, cast; (Hoph) be thrown, cast

- דֶּלֶת
  - door

- דַּעַת
  - knowledge, understanding, ability

- הָמוֹן
  - multitude, crowd, sound, roar

- זְרוֹעַ
  - (fs) arm, forearm; (metaphorically) strength or power

- כְּרוּב
  - cherub

- כֶּרֶם
  - vineyard

- The most important diagnostic features for the strong verb of the Piel stem include: (1) Vocal Shewa under all Imperfect preformatives and Participle prefixes; (2) Pathach under the first root consonant of every conjugation except the Perfect; and (3) Daghesh Forte in the second root consonant of every form in every conjugation. Though not considered to be diagnostic, it is helpful to note the Tsere stem vowel throughout the conjugations.

- The Piel stem may be used to express an *intensive* type of action with an *active* voice. In other words, the simple action of the Qal stem will take on some type of intensive nuance in the Piel stem.

- The *factitive* use of the Piel makes an intransitive Qal verb transitive. In other words, if a Qal verb is intransitive (cannot take a direct object), it will become transitive (can take a direct object) in the Piel stem.

- Verbs that are derived from a noun or adjective are often inflected in the Piel stem, not the Qal. When this occurs, the type of verbal action is simple and not intensive.

- The *iterative* action of the Piel expresses the nuance of repeated action. This use occurs primarily with verbs that express physical movement, effort, or voice projection. This type of action is often difficult to translate into English.

- Some verbs in the Piel stem are translated just like verbs in the Qal. This is frequently the case with verbal roots that are common in the Piel stem but are not attested (or rarely attested) in the Qal.

- Note that the Daghesh Forte in the second consonant of the verbal root will also characterize the strong verb inflections of the Pual and Hithpael stems.

- Note the distinctive מ prefix in the forms of the Piel Participle. This same prefix also occurs with the Participles of the Hiphil, Hophal, Hithpael, and Pual stems.

Quiz

1. (T/F) The Piel stem is used to express an intensive type of action with a passive voice.

2. What are the uses of the Piel stem?

    a) Intensive, Reciprocal, Denominative, Iterative
    b) Intensive, Factitive, Denominative, Reflexive
    c) Intensive, Factitive, Denominative, Iterative
    d) Intensive, Factitive, Declarative, Iterative

3. Which of the following most accurately represents the Piel Perfect Strong Verb diagnostics?

    a) קִטֵּל
    b) קַטֵּל
    c) קִטֵּל
    d) קַטֵּל

4. Parse: אֲדַבֵּר

    a) Piel Perfect 1cs from דבר
    b) Niphal Imperfect 1cs from דבר
    c) Qal Imperfect 1cs from דבר
    d) Piel Imperfect 1cs from דבר

5. Which of the following most accurately represents the Piel Imperfect Strong Verb diagnostics?

    a) יְקַטֵּל
    b) יְקַטֵּל
    c) יְקְטֵל
    d) יְקַטֵּל

6. (T/F) In the Infinitive Absolute, the Piel stem uses an e-class stem vowel.

7. Translate: אֶל־הָעֲבָדִים הַמְּלָכִים דִּבְּרוּ

   a) The king's words were to the servants
   b) The kings spoke to the servant
   c) The king spoke to the servants
   d) The kings spoke to the servants

8. What diagnostic indicates that the Piel stem מְדַבֵּר is a Participle?

   a) The Pathach under the first root consonant
   b) The Shewa under the מ
   c) The מ Preformative
   d) The Daghesh Forte in the second root consonant

9. Parse: לַמֵּד

   a) Piel Imperative 2ms from למד
   b) Piel Infinitive Construct from למד
   c) Piel Infinitive Absolute from למד
   d) Any of the above

10. Translate: בַּקֵּשׁ תְּפִלָּה

   a) You (mp) seek prayer!
   b) You (ms) will seek prayer
   c) You (ms) seek prayer!
   d) You (mp) will seek prayer

CHAPTER 31

The Piel Stem
Weak Verbs

You Should Know

- אָוֶן
  - iniquity, wickedness, evildoer

- אוֹצָר
  - treasure, treasury, storehouse

- אוֹת
  - sign, mark, pledge

- גּוֹרָל
  - lot, portion, allotment

- חוֹמָה
  - wall

- יְשׁוּעָה
  - salvation, help, deliverance

- מִקְנֶה
  - cattle, livestock, property

- מִשְׁמֶרֶת
  - watch, guard, responsibility

- נֶגַע
  - plague, affliction

- צַר
  - adversary, enemy

- Most weak verbs in Piel stem maintain the diagnostic features of the strong verb. It is only II-Guttural weak verbs that exhibit any major changes in spelling.

- The weak verb classes III-ח/ע, III-א, III-ה, and Geminate are given for your study, but you will observe that all of the strong verb diagnostics are preserved in each weak verb class.

- Once again, the major diagnostic features of the Piel stem include: (1) Daghesh Forte in the second root consonant; (2) Pathach under the first consonant of the verbal root in every conjugation except the Perfect; and (3) Vocal Shewa under all Imperfect preformatives and Participle prefixes.

- The only weak verbs to experience any significant change in these diagnostics are II-Guttural weak verbs.

Quiz

1. בֵּעֲרוּ: What has happened to the diagnostic Daghesh Forte in the second root consonant of this Piel Perfect 3cp verb?
   a) The guttural rejected it resulting in virtual doubling
   b) The guttural rejected it resulting in compensatory lengthening
   c) Gutturals prefer a-class vowels
   d) A Daghesh Forte cannot go above Hateph vowels

2. Parse: מַלֵּא
   a) Piel Imperative 2ms from מלא
   b) Piel Infinitive Construct from מלא
   c) Piel Infinitive Absolute מלא
   d) Any of the above

3. Parse: מְמַלְּאוֹת
   a) Piel Participle fp from מלא
   b) Piel Participle fs from מלא
   c) Niphal Participle fp from מלא
   d) Niphal Participle fs from מלא

4. Translate: וַיְחַזֵּק יְהוָה אֶת־לֵב פַּרְעֹה

    a) Yahweh hardened the heart of Pharoah
    b) And Yahweh hardened the heart of Pharoah
    c) Yahweh hardened Pharoah with his heart
    d) And Yahweh hardened Pharoah with his heart

5. Parse: וַיְחַזֵּק
    a) Piel Imperfect 3ms from חזק
    b) Piel Imperfect 3ms from חזק + Waw Consecutive
    c) Piel Imperfect 3mp from חזק
    d) Piel Imperfect 3mp from חזק + Waw Consecutive

6. מְבָרֵךְ: What has happened to the diagnostic Daghesh Forte in the second root consonant of this Piel ms participle?
    a) The guttural rejected it resulting in virtual doubling
    b) The guttural rejected it resulting in compensatory lengthening
    c) Gutturals prefer a-class vowels
    d) A Daghesh Forte cannot go above Hateph vowels

7. Parse: בְּעַרְתֶּם
    a) Qal Perfect 2mp from בער
    b) Niphal Perfect 2mp from בער
    c) Piel Perfect 2mp from בער
    d) Piel Imperfect 2mp from בער

8. Parse: יְנַחֵם
    a) Piel Imperfect 3ms from נחם
    b) Piel Imperfect 3cp from נחם
    c) Piel Imperative 2ms from נחם
    d) Piel Perfect 3cp from נחם

9. Parse: תִּקַּח
    a) Piel Perfect 3ms from תקח
    b) Piel Perfect 3ms from לקח
    c) Qal Perfect 3ms from לקח
    d) Qal Perfect 2ms from לקח

10. (T/F) הִלֵּל: The Daghesh Forte in the second root letter of this Geminate Piel Perfect 3ms is the geminate consonant.

CHAPTER 32

The Pual Stem Strong Verbs

You Should Know

- יָדָה
  - (Hi) to thank, praise, confess; (Hith) confess

- נָבַט
  - (Hi) to look (at or out), gaze, behold

- פָּלָא
  - (Ni) to be extraordinary, wonderful; (Hi) do something wonderful

- רִיב
  - (Q) to strive, contend, quarrel, dispute, conduct a legal case

- שִׁית
  - (Q) to set, put, place, set one's mind to

- אֶרֶז
  - cedar

- פֵּאָה
  - corner, side, edge

- צוּר
  - rock, boulder

- קֶרֶן
  - horn

- קֶשֶׁת
  - bow, weapon

- The most significant diagnostic features of the Pual stem include: (1) Vocal Shewa under all Imperfect preformatives and Participle prefixes; (2) Qibbuts under the first root consonant of every form; and (3) Daghesh Forte in the second root consonant of every form.

- The first and third diagnostic features are identical to the Piel stem. Therefore, the second diagnostic feature (Qibbuts under the first root consonant) will distinguish Pual forms from Piel forms. Given the infrequency of certain Pual forms, we will study only the Perfect, Imperfect, and Participle.

- The Pual stem is the passive of the Piel stem. The Pual stem may be used, therefore, to express an *intensive* type of action with a *passive* voice.

- For example, the Piel Perfect verb שִׁבֵּר means "he smashed." The Pual form would be שֻׁבַּר and it may be translated "he (it) was smashed." Notice how a form of the English verb "to be" (was) is used to make the translation passive. Also, like the Piel, the Pual may be factitive, denominative, or iterative.

- The important diagnostic feature is Qibbuts under the first consonant of the verbal root in every form (קֻטַּל). This feature distinguishes the Pual Perfect from the Piel Perfect.

Quiz

1. (T/F) The Pual stem is used to express an intensive action with a passive voice.

2. Identify the correct diagnostic pattern for the Pual Perfect Strong Verb.

   a) קְטַל
   b) קֻטֶּל
   c) קֻטַּל
   d) קוּטַל

3. Parse: סֻפַּר

   a) Piel Perfect 3ms from ספר

   b) Pual Perfect 3ms from ספר

   c) Piel Imperative 2ms from ספר

   d) Pual Imperative 2ms from ספר

4. Identify the correct diagnostic pattern for the Pual Imperfect Strong Verb.

   a) יְקַטַל

   b) יְקֻטַּל

   c) יְקוּטַּל

   d) יְקַטַּל

5. Identify the correct diagnostic pattern for the Pual Imperative Strong Verb.

   a) קוּטַל

   b) קֻטַּל

   c) קוֹטַּל

   d) There isn't one

6. Parse: גֻּדְּלוּ

   a) Piel Perfect 3cp from גדל

   b) Pual Perfect 3cp from גדל

   c) Piel Imperative 2ms from גדל

   d) Pual Imperative 2ms from גדל

7. Translate: צִדְקוֹ וְחַסְדּוֹ יְבֻקְּשׁוּ

   a) His righteousness and his faithfulness will be sought

   b) I will seek his righteousness and his faithfulness

   c) You (mp) seek his righteousness and his faithfulness

   d) His righteousness and his faithfulness will be sought by me

8. Identify the correct diagnostic pattern for the Pual Participle Strong Verb.

   a) קֻטַּל

   b) מְקוּטָּל

   c) מְקֻטָּל

   d) מְקַטָּל

9. Translate: הַנָּבִיא אֶת־דִּבְרֵי הַמֶּלֶךְ דִּבֶּר

   a) The word of the king was spoken by the prophet
   b) The prophet spoke the words of the king
   c) The prophet spoke the word of the king
   d) The words of the king were spoken by the prophet

10. (T/F) The Piel and Pual stems both have a Daghesh Forte in the second root letter and a מ prefix in the participle form.

CHAPTER 33

The Pual Stem
Weak Verbs

You Should Know

- לִין
  - (Q) to remain overnight, spend the night

- מָשַׁח
  - (Q) to smear (with a liquid, oil or dye), anoint (with oil)

- עָנָה
  - (Q) to be afflicted, humbled; (Pi) afflict, oppress, humiliate, violate

- רָכַב
  - (Q) to ride, mount and ride; (Hi) cause or make to ride

- שָׁבַת
  - (Q) to stop, cease, rest; (Hi) put an end to, remove, put away

- בֶּטֶן
  - belly, stomach, womb

- גִּבְעָה
  - hill

- הֶבֶל
  - vanity, futility, breath

- חֶרְפָּה
  - reproach, disgrace, shame

- מִזְרָח
  - east, sunrise

- Once again, the diagnostic features of the Pual stem include: (1) Qibbuts under the first root consonant of every form; (2) Daghesh Forte in the second root consonant of every form; and (3) Vocal Shewa under all Imperfect preformatives and Participle prefixes.

- Remember that the Qibbuts under the first root consonant distinguishes the Pual from the Piel. Also, like the Piel, only II-Guttural weak verbs exhibit any significant changes in the Pual.

- As in the Piel stem, most Pual weak verbs maintain the strong verb diagnostics. Only II-Guttural verbs exhibit significant changes in the Pual. Both the III-א and III-ה verb classes maintain all of the Pual strong verb diagnostics.

- All of the Pual strong verb diagnostics are present in this weak verb class, except the Daghesh Forte in the second root consonant. This verb exhibits virtual doubling.

Quiz

1. בֹּרַךְ: What has happened to the Qibbuts under the first root consonant and the diagnostic Daghesh Forte in the 2nd root consonant of this Pual Perfect 3ms verb?

   a) The Daghesh Forte was rejected resulting in virtual doubling
   b) The Daghesh Forte simply dropped out
   c) The Daghesh Forte was rejected resulting in compensatory lengthening
   d) The Qibbuts lengthened because open pretonic syllables require long vowels

2. Parse: מֻלֵּאתִי
   a) Pual Imperfect 1cs from מלא
   b) Piel Perfect 1cs from מלא
   c) Piel Imperfect 1cs from מלא
   d) Pual Perfect 1cs from מלא

3. Parse: מְמֻלָּאִים

   a) Pual Participle ms from מלא

   b) Piel Participle ms from מלא

   c) Pual Participle mp from מלא

   d) Piel Participle mp from מלא

4. Translate: יְבֹרַךְ אָבִיהוּ

   a) He will bless his father

   b) His father will be blessed

   c) His father would be blessed

   d) His father will bless him

5. יְנֻחַם: What has happened to the expected Daghesh Forte of this Pual Imperfect verb form?

   a) It has been rejected by the guttural and lengthened to Holem

   b) It has been rejected by the guttural and lengthened to Holem Waw

   c) It has been rejected by the guttural and lengthened to Qibbuts

   d) It has been rejected by the guttural resulting in virtual doubling

6. Translate: גֻּלֵּינוּ

   a) We will be uncovered

   b) We will uncover

   c) We were uncovered

   d) We uncovered

7. Parse: בֹּעַרְתֶּם

   a) Pual Perfect 2mp בער

   b) Piel Perfect 2mp בער

   c) Pual Perfect 2ms בער

   d) Piel Perfect 2ms בער

8. Parse: נַחֵם

   a) Piel Imperative 2ms from נחם

   b) Piel Infinitive Construct from נחם

   c) Pual Infinitive Absolute from נחם

   d) Both A and B

9. Parse: מְבֹרְכָיו

   a) Pual Participle mp from ברך

   b) Pual Participle ms from ברך

   c) Pual Participle mp from רכה

   d) Pual Participle mp from ברך with 3ms suffix

10. Translate: צִדְקוֹ וְחַסְדּוֹ יִמָּצֵא

   a) He found his righteousness and faithfulness

   b) His righteousness and faithfulness will be found

   c) He will find his righteousness and faithfulness

   d) His righteousness and faithfulness was found

CHAPTER 34

The Hithpael Stem Strong Verbs

You Should Know

- פָּלַל
  - (Hith) to pray, make intercession
- תָּקַע
  - (Q) to drive or thrust (weapon into a person), pitch (tent), blow (trumpet), clap one's hands
- אוֹר
  - light, daylight, sunshine
- לָשׁוֹן
  - tongue, language
- מִקְדָּשׁ
  - sanctuary
- עוֹף
  - flying creatures, birds, insects
- עֵז
  - goat, goat's hair
- פְּרִי
  - fruit, offspring
- קִיר
  - wall

- רֶכֶב

  - chariot, (coll) chariots or chariot riders

- In every form of every Hithpael strong verb conjugation, there is a Pathach under the first consonant of the verbal root and a Daghesh Forte in the second consonant of the verbal root.

- In the Perfect, Imperative, Infinitive Construct, and Infinitive Absolute, the prefix is הִת.

- The preformatives for the Imperfect are יִת, תִּת, אֶת, or נִת, and the prefix for the Participle is מִת. These distinctive preformatives and prefixes make the Hithpael stem easy to identify with most verbs.

- Metathesis is a term used to describe the transposition of two contiguous (side-by-side) consonants in order to smooth out a word's pronunciation. Whenever the ת of a Hithpael prefix or preformative precedes verbal roots beginning with שׁ, צ, ס, or שׂ (sibilant or "s" sound consonants), the two consonants will switch places.

- Finally, if a verbal root begins with ט, ז, ד, or ת, the ת of the Hithpael preformative or prefix will assimilate into the first consonant of the verbal root and remain as a Daghesh Forte.

Quiz

1. What kind of verbal *action* is expressed in the Hithpael stem?
   - a) Simple
   - b) Intensive
   - c) Causitive
   - d) Reflexive

2. Identify the correct representation of the Hithpael Strong Verb Diagnostics.
   - a) הִתְקַטֵּל
   - b) הִתְקַטֵּל
   - c) הִתְקְטֵּל
   - d) הָתְקַטֵּל

3. (T/F) In the Hithpael Imperfect, the ה of the Hithpael gets replaced by the Imperfect Preformative Consonant, while all other diagnostic features remain.

4. Parse: הִתְכַּתֵּב
   a) Hithpael Imperative 2ms from כתב
   b) Hithpael Infinitive Construct from כתב
   c) Hithpael Infinitive Absolute from כתב
   d) All of the above

5. What are the uses of the Hithpael stem?
   a) Reciprocal, Denominative, Iterative, Simple
   b) Reciprocal, Reflexive, Simple, Intensive
   c) Intensive, Iterative, Passive, Simple
   d) Reciprocal, Intensive, Iterative, Simple

6. What do the Piel, Pual, and Hithpael stems have in common?
   a) Vocal shewa under the Preformative
   b) Pathach Stem vowel
   c) Daghesh Forte in the second root letter
   d) All of the above

7. הִשְׁתַּמֵּר: What explains why the Taw appears to have switched places with the Shin in this Hithpael Perfect 3ms verb?
   a) Closed unaccented syllables prefer short vowels.
   b) Metathesis
   c) sknmlwy
   d) This spelling is unique to שמר.

8. Which Hebrew Consonants initiate Metathesis?
   a) שׁ שׂ כ נ מ ל ו י
   b) ב ג ד כ פ ת
   c) ז ד ט ת
   d) ס שׁ שׂ צ

9. הִדַּבֵּר: What is the Daghesh in the ד of this Hithpael verb form?
   a) The Taw of the Hithpael Stem assimilated as a Daghesh Lene
   b) The Taw of the Hithpael Stem assimilated as a Daghesh Forte

c) Conjunctive Daghesh
d) A Daghesh Lene motivated by the presence of a *begadkephat* letter

10. Which Hebrew consonants initiate the assimilation of the Taw in the Hithpael diagnostics into the following consonant as a Daghesh Forte?

a) שׁשׂכנמלוי
b) בגדכפת
c) זדטת
d) סשׁשׂצ

CHAPTER 35

The Hithpael Stem Weak Verbs

You Should Know

- חָוָה
  - (Hishtaphel) to bow down, worship

- בָּמָה
  - (cultic) high place, sacred hill

- בַּרְזֶל
  - iron

- כֶּבֶשׂ
  - lamb, sheep

- עֵמֶק
  - valley, plain

- צָרָה
  - distress, anxiety, trouble

- רָעָב
  - famine, hunger

- שׁוֹר
  - ox, bull, cow

- שֻׁלְחָן
  - table

- תְּפִלָּה

  – prayer

- It is only the II-Guttural class of weak verbs that exhibits significant variation from the strong verb diagnostics. A guttural consonant in second root position will reject the expected Daghesh Forte. The guttural's rejection of the Daghesh Forte results in either virtual doubling or compensatory lengthening.

- Most verbs in the Geminate weak verb class retain all of the Hithpael strong verb diagnostics.

- All of the strong verb diagnostics are retained in in the Hithpael forms of III-ה verbs. The endings that are present on these III-ה Hithpael conjugations are the same ones that were seen on the Qal and all of the other derived stems previously studied.

- A guttural consonant in second root position will reject the expected Daghesh Forte. The guttural's rejection of the Daghesh Forte results in either virtual doubling or compensatory lengthening (31.6, 33.4). Hithpael II-Guttural verbs respond in the same two ways.

- With the exception of the absence of the Daghesh Forte in the second consonant of the verbal root, all of the other strong verb diagnostics are retained.

Quiz

1. (T/F) With Geminate verbs in the Hithpael Stem, the geminate consonant will assimilate as a Daghesh Forte.

2. Parse: תִּתְנַחֲלוּ
   a) Hithpael Imperfect 2mp from נחל
   b) Hithpael Perfect 3ms from נחל with 3ms suffix
   c) Hithpael Imperfect 3mp from נחל
   d) Hithpael Perfect 3ms from נחל

3. יִתְבָּרֶךְ: Why is there a Qamets under the first root consonant instead of the expected Pathach in this Hithpael Imperfect verb?

   a) Compensatory Lengthening by way of rejection of the Daghesh
      Forte by ר
   b) Vowel reduction by way of rejection of the Daghesh Forte by ר
   c) Open pretonic syllables require a long vowel.
   d) Both A and C

4. What do the Piel, Pual, Hiphil, Hophal, and Hithpael stems all
have in common?

   a) Daghesh Forte in the second root letter
   b) Hireq or Qamets under the first root consonant
   c) A prefixed ה in every conjugation
   d) A diagnostic מ in the Participle

5. (T/F) The Hithpael stem has the only II-Guttural class of weak verbs
that exhibits significant variation from the strong verb diagnostics.

6. What is the best translation of the word בֶּבֶשׂ?

   a) Table
   b) Valley, plain
   c) Ox, bull, cow
   d) Lamb, sheep

7. Parse: יִתְהַלֵּל

   a) Qal Imperfect 3ms from תהל
   b) Hithpael Imperfect 3mp from הלל
   c) Hithpael Imperfect 3ms from הלל
   d) Piel Imperfect 3ms from תהל

8. Parse: מְתְנַבְּאוֹת

   a) Hithpael Participle fs from נבא
   b) Hithpael Infinitive Absolute from נבא
   c) Hithpael Participle fp from נבא
   d) Hithpael Infinitive Construct from נבא

9. Parse: הִתְעַנּוֹת

   a) Hithpael Participle fs from ענו
   b) Hithpael Perfect 2fp from ענה
   c) Hithpael Participle fp from ענה
   d) Hithpael Infinitive Construct from ענה

10. Parse: תִּשְׁתַּפֵּךְ

   a) Hithpael Imperfect 3fs from שפך

   b) Hithpael Imperfect 2ms from שפך

   c) Hithpael Imperfect 3fs from שתפ

   d) Either A or B

Notes